# DIGITAL PASSPORT

## YOUR PASS TO A PROMISING CAREER IN DIGITAL MARKETING

D1598259

**Publishing Info and Copyright**

## © 2018 BY OMNICORE

First Edition - January 2018

ISBN 978-0-692-99155-8

All rights reserved.

# DISCLAIMER

This book is to be used for information that helps aspiring digital marketers obtain employment and a fruitful career in digital marketing. However, the information provided in this book is to be considered as advice, not a guarantee of success. All information provided herein is for the sake of information and educational purposes only.

Additionally, the book does not contain legal, financial, tax, or other professional advice that requires the services of a pertinent industry professional. The material provided herein is offered without warranty of any kind. The author and publisher make no representation or warranty regarding the accuracy, completeness, or applicability of the book's contents and information. Information in the book may be updated without notice at any time, and the author and publisher make no representation about the suitability of the book's information for any purpose.

The author and publisher have used their best efforts in preparing the book material. Every effort has been made to ensure complete accuracy of the book's content and material, but errors and omissions may have occurred. The author and publisher make no claim that the book is comprehensive in nature, as the book is the opinion of the author and publisher. Some readers may wish to consult additional digital marketing books and sources for further advice.

Links, products and authors listed in the book are owned and operated by third parties. The author and publisher do not have any affiliation with these individuals and have no control over the information provided by these sites and other media. Links and references included in the book are exclusively for reference purposes.

The book and its information are not authorized or endorsed by Google, Amazon, Facebook, or any other firm, company or entity mentioned in the book.

# ABOUT THE AUTHOR

Hafiz Muhammad Ali is an Internet Entrepreneur and the founder of Omnicore Group, a company that has built a portfolio of successful online businesses across advertising, consumer reviews, and brain nutrition.

He has received a MSc degree in Digital Marketing Leadership from The University of Aberdeen and training from Digital Marketing Institute, Google, and MarketMotive.

Beyond his role as a Founder, Advisor, and CEO to several companies, he is a certified life coach from University of Cambridge, and a regular contributor at Entrepreneur.com.

Now, he is passing on what he has learned to the benefit of aspiring digital marketing job seekers in the form of *Digital Passport: Your Pass to a Promising Career in Digital Marketing.*

To contact Hafiz Muhammad, contact him via the following resources: **hello@hafizmuhammadali.com**

# DIGITAL MARKETING CAREER ASSESSMENT TEST

Industry's first digital marketing career test looks at your unique mix of personality characteristics, aptitude, and abilities. By using this information, our algorithm tells you which digital marketing roles best fit you.

This personalized approach helps you: Save Time and Frustration. Earn More Money. Feel Fulfilled and Happy. You can Win Our Scholarship to Become a Certified Digital Marketer.

Digital Ladder is an advance unbiased test designed by Hafiz who is digital marketing career and leadership coach and expert Psychologist specialized in Psychoanalysis & Neuro Linguistic Programing (NLP).

Use the discount code below to get 50% off your
**Digital Ladder - Digital Marketing Psychometric Test**

DIGIPASSBOOK50%

Visit **www.hafizmuhammadali.com/digital-ladder/**
to learn more.

# DEDICATION

To all aspiring digital marketers...

# TABLE OF CONTENTS

Chapter 1: Digital Marketing (And Your) Time Is Now — PG. 2 →

Chapter 2: Choosing eCommerce As a Launchpad to a Digital Marketing Career — PG. 12 →

Chapter 3: Mobile Has Paved the Way for Digital Marketing Career Opportunities — PG. 30 →

Chapter 4: Social Media Stands to Play a Large Role in Digital Marketing's Future — PG. 50 →

Chapter 5: For the Tech-Savvy Digital Marketer, a Web Analytics Career Awaits — PG. 66 →

Chapter 6: Searching for a Digital Marketing Career? Consider Search Marketing — PG. 84 →

Chapter 7: Email Aged Like Fine Wine, and It Still Has an Important Part to Play in the Future of Digital Marketing — PG. 102 →

Chapter 8: Making the Pitch for a Career in Digital Marketing Sales — PG. 120 →

Chapter 9: SEO Continues to Be a Springboard Into the World of Digital Marketing — PG. 139 →

Chapter 10: Getting Noticed in a Crowded Digital Marketing Field — PG. 155 →

Chapter 11: How to Find the Perfect Digital Marketing Career — PG. 171 →

Chapter 12: Why Agency Life Is a Great Entry Point Into Digital Marketing — PG. 187 →

Chapter 13: A Career in Digital Marketing Is a Lifelong Educational Pursuit — PG. 195 →

**NOTES FROM THE AUTHOR**

# Your Rewarding Digital Marketing Career Starts With a First Step

*Don't wait until you are rea•y to take action. Instea•, take action to be rea•y.*
- Jensen Siaw

Without taking the first step in a journey, it is impossible to get to the ultimate destination. In your life journey, you are here reading this book right at this moment for a reason. You are considering a fulfilling new career in digital marketing. I have been in your shoes, as I too was once pondering what would come next for my future. I chose digital marketing, and I have never looked back. It has been a fulfilling experience, and I would choose it again in a heartbeat.

My name is Hafiz Muhammad Ali, and through humble beginnings, I have worked my way toward becoming Founder of Omnicore Group. While this is the result of my digital marketing journey, my career and story are far from over. The digital marketing world changes too fast to remain static for long, which is why I am constantly inspired and looking forward to what new changes this industry will bring my way.

Despite the constant changes looming in the future, allow me to take you back a few years to the start of my digital marketing career. The year is 2006, and I am just taking my first bold forays into the world of digital marketing. SEO experts and those trying to make a quick buck are swift in telling the aspiring marketer that success and fortune are sure to come quickly. Let me be the first to tell you that, truthfully, my early years brought no instant success. In fact, one may even describe those years as tough going.

Once I decided digital marketing would be my career, I aspired to make a difference in this field. Despite this unwavering desire, the success did not come overnight. If I could travel back in time and relay what I have learned in the years since, I would tell myself success does not come overnight or even in a year. Success in digital marketing requires constant learning, dedication, and hard work, which does not happen instantaneously. There is simply too much to learn, absorb, and implement for it to be otherwise.

Fortunately, I had passion to carry me through the tough times in those early years. By 2009, I met my friend Salman Aslam, who was about to graduate at the time. He was doing freelance work, and we talked about why I was not achieving the success I had hoped for. After many discussions about digital marketing, end users and the like, we decided to launch our own company, Omnicore. Unfortunately, we did not even have $100 for the domain registration! I borrowed $90 from a friend, and from there, we began the long grind of making a name for ourselves in this industry.

For two long years, Salman and I often worked 40 consecutive hours before crashing for four hours, and then doing it all over again. We were doing all the work ourselves, which included writing, website design, and website development. We read all the online resources and watched all the YouTube tutorials we could find, and yet, we did not have any clients in the first four months. Cynics and skeptics told us that without more capital and money invested, we would be wasting our time. These difficult times were the rare moments that I questioned pursuing my dream of making a difference in this field. Fortunately, both Salman and I were too dedicated to quit. Still, there were times when the cynics and skeptics almost convinced us.

Such was the case on one particularly long and difficult night in which I was most susceptible to quitting. I tossed and I turned, restless with frustration. I felt so far from reaching my goal of achieving a career in digital marketing. I could not sleep at all that night. Two more sleepless nights followed until three days had passed with no sleep or work. On this third night, I had an epiphany, one that has motivated me since.

I simply asked myself, "What do you want to do with your life after you give up on this dream?" There was no satisfying answer. I had worked so hard in this field because I wanted to make a difference in digital marketing. Nothing had changed in that regard. The only thing that left me dissatisfied was the slow path to success. This revelatory insight caused me to get out of bed with renewed passion and fervor, reinvigorated to work harder than ever.

I kept at this breakneck pace for five long months until we finally landed our first client, a French brand involved with the French industry. They trusted us with their digital marketing needs, and as a result, their return on investment (ROI) jumped from 5 to 23% in just three months. Seven years later, they are still our client. Even as Omnicore works with Top 500 Inc. companies today, we are eternally grateful for the chance that French brand gave to us when we were starting out.

I must also stress to you that my successes have never been mine alone. On my career journey, my friend Salman has been a trusted business partner, digital marketing expert, and motivational friend every step of the way. Thanks to his relentless enthusiasm and passion for digital marketing, I managed to overcome my contemplation for quitting. Today, he manages all Omnicore company affairs, all while suffering from muscular dystrophy. He overcame these hurdles as we worked to become successful entrepreneurs.

I tell you our story not to brag and certainly not to scare you away from digital marketing. Believe me when I tell you I look back on even the difficult years with fondness today. Rather, I tell you our story so you can better understand that living and breathing digital marketing each day is the best path toward sustained success. Since starting Omnicore, Salman and I have pursued excellence in this field with passion on a daily basis, save for a few dejected nights at our lowest moments. Passion and a belief in making a difference climbed out of that valley, giving us the success that helped us arrive to where we are today.

With this perspective and lived experience, I write to you at this critical time of career decision-making. Digital marketing has been my passion since Day One, and this is the most surefire way to succeed that I know. Perhaps you are wondering why digital marketing is so fulfilling to me, or perhaps you are wondering why you should strive to succeed in digital marketing when there are other career options available.

Digital marketing could allow you to earn a quality income and change the world. After all, the digital marketing careers are taking off because businesses and the world understand digital marketing has the potential to shape and improve the world in uniquely amazing ways. There is so much more to this field that I find valuable, however.

Beyond the big picture of changing the world, helping brands grow, and improving people's daily lives, I love the little benefits of digital marketing that are not immediately obvious, such as digital marketing's potential to make anyone who chooses this career path a better person. Having a great job is one thing, but how many jobs challenge you to improve the way you think and interact with your world? The non-stop learning curve of this field will keep you on your toes and challenge you to become an inquisitive and adaptive person. This process will humble you and help you grow wiser in the process. In the spirit of Socrates' famous thoughts on knowledge, this journey will help you see how little you know while inspiring personal growth.

Digital marketing has challenged me to constantly seek out more knowledge and insight, which often has meant relying on the advice and expertise of respected industry professionals. In the process, I have grown to enjoy a successful digital marketing career, and now it is my hope to pass on all that I have learned to you, the reader.

I owe digital marketing greatly for enabling me to have a fulfilling career, which is why I am writing this book—to pass down the knowledge I have obtained. Whether it is passing on the skills obtained from years of professional experience, or education from the MSc in Digital Marketing Leadership and various certifications, know that you are reading information gathered by a lifelong student. Success in this field depends on constant learning and adaptation, and my firsthand education, training, and experience should give you the knowledge needed to make an informed decision on whether this career path is right for you.

Over the years, I have been blessed with the opportunity to share my accumulated knowledge with individuals just like you who are curious about a career in this field. The lessons I share are come from practical experience, knowledge that helps me ensure my company will be ready to respond to any change in the industry. My hope is that this book will inform, educate, and inspire you to pursue a career in the incredible industry we call digital marketing. If you choose to take the first steps into your digital marketing journey, I would like to leave you with a few practical words of advice.

First, fully commit to putting your whole heart into pursuing this dream. You will get as much out of this field as you put into it. If you put all of yourself into this pursuit, I am confident you will find a way to achieve your dreams, and you may even surprise yourself with just how far you are able to go in your career.

Second, stay passionate. While you will certainly not be bored by a career in the ever-changing digital marketing field, make sure you remain a lifelong student who is committed to learning. Keeping this lifelong learning approach at the forefront of everything you do as a digital marketer ensures you will not be left behind as the industry continues its evolution.

Finally, do not be afraid to step up and take on challenges. In the following chapters, you will find that advancing in some areas of digital marketing will require you to embrace difficult concepts and weighty ideas that will challenge you. Never back down from any challenge because it seems too difficult. What may seem difficult or demanding in print is in fact just an opportunity waiting to be seized in reality. If you read about a job opportunity in this book that seems perfect for your personality and skillset, do not shy away from pursuing that job because of what you perceive to be difficult. This book will provide you with the knowledge and resources you will need to turn career goals and a vision into a real and rewarding digital marketing career.

# CHAPTER SUMMARIES

- **Chapter 1: "Digital Marketing (and your) Time is Now"** explores why the time is right to take the first bold steps toward an exciting career in digital marketing. The chapter also explains key concepts concerning why digital marketers are in high demand and what it takes to succeed in the field.

- **Chapter 2: "Choosing eCommerce as a Launchpad to a Digital Marketing Career"** takes a closer look at how digital marketing is used in the ever-growing space of eCommerce. Influential case studies highlight why the future of retail is online, while also taking a closer look at what it takes to succeed in eCommerce.

- **Chapter 3: "Mobile Has Paved the Way for Digital Marketing Career Opportunities"** delves into how smartphones and mobile technology have revolutionized the world and the opportunities within digital marketing. Mastering mobile is essential to digital marketing success, and this chapter explains why and highlights available career options in the field.

- **Chapter 4: "Social Media Stands to Play a Large Role in Digital Marketing's Future"** discusses social media's influence on marketing that has translated into consumers preferring social, engaged brands. Plenty of digital marketing jobs are available in this field, and this chapter lets you know the skills you will need to land one of these desirable positions.

- **Chapter 5: "For the Tech-Savvy Digital Marketer, a Web Analytics Career Awaits"** investigates how a digital analytics professional can make sense of petabytes of data and leverage it into actionable insight. Anyone who enthusiastically crunches numbers will find much to love about this field, and this chapter gives aspiring job seekers the tools needed to stand out in a job search.

- **Chapter 6: "Searching for a Digital Marketing Career? Consider Search Marketing"** explains the significant potential in search marketing, a field that sees top brands spend billions on this form of advertising.

- **Chapter 7: "Email Aged Like Fine Wine, and It Still Has an Important Part to Play in the Future of Digital Marketing"** highlights why email is a technology that will continue to play a major role in digital marketing's future and evolution. Readers will learn about the skills needed to excel in this area of digital marketing.

- **Chapter 8: "Making the Pitch for a Career in Digital Marketing Sales"** shows how digital marketing and the role of the salesperson are closely intertwined. The chapter takes an in-depth look at the traits of the successful digital marketing salesperson.

- **Chapter 9: "SEO Continues to Be a Springboard into the World of Digital Marketing"** explains why SEO continues to be a significant force in digital marketing and will be for years to come. SEO success requires adapting to the constant change, and this chapter prepares readers how to do just that.

- **Chapter 10: "Getting Noticed in a Crowded Digital Marketing Field"** helps aspiring marketers grasp what it takes to get positive attention from employers in this increasingly crowded field. Tips and case studies combine to make this a chapter that makes essential reading for future digital marketers.

- **Chapter 11: "How to Find the Perfect Digital Marketing Career"** gives you the tools to locate where digital marketing jobs are posted. From job boards to social media and recruiters, this chapter leaves no stone left unturned, giving readers a wealth of options and case studies that show how to successfully conduct a digital marketing job search.

- **Chapter 12: "Why Agency Life is a Great Entry Point into Digital Marketing"** focuses on why agencies are a perfect entry-level landing spot for advancing a digital marketing career. From finding the right entry-level role to climbing the corporate ladder, this chapter gives a detailed look at agency life.

- **Chapter 13: "A Career in Digital Marketing Is a Lifelong Educational Pursuit"** explains why being a lifelong learner is critical for sustaining success in digital marketing. The chapter provides a comprehensive look at some of the best educational courses and university programs to advance digital marketing knowledge.

# 01

///////////////////////////////////////////////////////////

## DIGITAL MARKETING (AND YOUR) TIME IS NOW

---

### WHAT YOU WILL LEARN IN THIS CHAPTER:

- Why the Future of Digital Marketing Is Now
- Trends Prove the Need for Skilled Marketers
- How Businesses Benefit From Hiring Digital Marketers
- Why a Digital Marketing Career is so Rewarding
- What You Will Need to Succeed in This Career Path

John grabs his phone on his way out the door, as he never leaves home without it. A quick check of his email, browsing social media, visiting a mobile website, or using his favorite app can be all it takes to make a purchase. The immediacy of the digital world at John's fingertips provides him with an unparalleled opportunity to connect with brands and purchase their products. "John" is simply one of billions of people who are now able to buy the products they need within seconds before sharing their opinions on those products with the world.

If the product is digital, John may be using the very product he purchased minutes or even seconds later. The rise of the internet, smartphones, social media and similarly exciting digital technologies have quite simply transformed the world in which we live, ensuring most of us make purchases just like John. This transformation has been made possible thanks to digital marketing. If a career in digital marketing is something you have been considering or you are simply interested in the industry's potential, you should understand now is the time to jump into this ever-expanding field. Do not just take my word for it; let the numbers, facts, and data speak for themselves. According to a survey of marketing executives conducted by Gartner, Inc., digital marketing is the main catalyst behind the climbing marketing budgets of companies.

The Gartner CMO Spend Survey 2016-2017 shows that marketing leaders spent more on websites, digital commerce, and digital advertising than any other category. Effectively, Gartner concludes that "while digital has become integral to all marketing activities, pure digital marketing investments remain a top priority." Of the 51% of companies planning to increase their digital marketing budget, the average planned increase was a robust 17%.

As the line between traditional marketing and digital marketing continues to narrow, expect companies to continue the expansion of their digital marketing budgets. By 2020, the digital needs of companies are expected to translate into 150,000 digital jobs by 2020. If such a promising forecast sounds too good to be true, your intuition is correct. While there are many jobs available in digital marketing, there are many happy digital marketers in this industry. According to Digiday's State of the Industry Survey on Job Satisfaction, well more than three in four digital marketers indicated they are happy or satisfied at their current job. Despite the fact there are hundreds of thousands of jobs available in promising digital marketing sectors, the truth of the matter is few people have the skills to fill those jobs. That is part of the value of this book.

The future of digital marketing is here, but you need the necessary knowledge and resources to know how to seize these fulfilling career opportunities. Rest assured that small and midsized businesses will not rest on their laurels. They are going to have to search for ways to bridge the skills gap, ensuring they can hire the employees they need. These corporations understand that the lack of skilled digital marketing employees inhibits company growth. With the resources in this book, you will have the knowledge needed to become a valuable asset for these companies.

By understanding the "ins and outs" of each field of digital marketing, you will be well positioned to find the right job fit for you and obtain the necessary skills to stand out in your chosen field. To fully dive into the future of digital marketing, it is important to highlight why companies need digital marketing professionals in the first place.

## WHY COMPANIES NEED DIGITAL MARKETERS

Digital marketing, quite simply, has revolutionized the way a business connects with its target market and customer base. Companies that choose not to tap into this revolution will be left behind by their competitors. As a result, many of the reasons why digital marketing's time is now stems from the fact businesses are competitive entities, first and foremost. The companies that best utilize the potential of digital marketing enjoy a distinct advantage over their peers in a respective industry.

Take, for example, the television industry. Evidence indicates that digital adspend is forecasted to exceed $113 billion in 2020, which should dramatically outpace the $77.93 billion in TV spending that year. In fact, digital adspend has already surpassed TV ad spending for the first time in 2016. Digital adspend saw more than $72 billion in revenue for 2016, whereas TV captured roughly $71.3 billion in revenue.

The reason for this shift is the fact that linear television is declining, as viewers increasingly look toward on-demand entertainment and digital streaming solutions like Netflix, HBO GO, and even YouTube, with its on demand service, YouTube Red. Further, two-thirds of digital advertising spending will be on mobile devices, which will only create the need for more digital marketing jobs in the mobile marketing sectors.

The TV advertising shift is just one of many industry evolutions making a move towards digital marketing. This is not a new trend, either. Chief marketing officers were prepared to declare 2013 the so-called "Year of Digital." More than 500 top marketers were surveyed, and these leading chief marketing officers saw that the future of digital marketing was rapidly approaching. These top marketers and industry influencers indicated they were already spending a larger percentage of their marketing budgets on digital marketing, and they also indicated that digital marketing was rapidly gaining on traditional marketing approaches.

As part of this 2013 survey, the chief marketing officers were asked about their future hiring plans within their companies. Half were planning to hire new digital marketing talent even in 2013, indicating that finding job seekers with proven digital expertise and qualifications was a top priority for these companies. While these experts believed that 2013 was the year when digital marketing truly took flight, the job market is even brighter today. This year you will be hard pressed to find a job description of a marketing position that does not require at least some familiarity with digital platforms and digital marketing strategies. Expect that trend to only increase in the years ahead.

In short, companies need digital marketers because they cannot afford to be left behind by the industry's move toward digital. If there is one point to take away from all this data, it is the fact that companies crave job candidates with solid and proven digital marketing skills and credentials.

With this knowledge in mind, you may be wondering why you should consider a career in digital marketing. Fortunately, there are many reasons why a digital marketing career is so fulfilling, and many of these reasons will likely resonate with you.

# WHY DIGITAL MARKETING CAREER IS A REWARDING ENDEAVOR

Digital marketing is a field that provides constant excitement, given that brands have to remain innovative and cutting edge in order to stay relevant. Because of this competition, the industry is constantly changing and reshaping the way marketing works. For one thing, digital marketing has led to a more direct connection between the brand and consumer than ever before. With TV and print ads, marketers had to hope they had the consumer's attention, as opposed to airing a commercial to an empty living room as the viewer left for a snack in the kitchen. Digital marketing is targeted, allowing brands to interact directly with their target audience on social media and other platforms, such as on a mobile device that consumers take with them everywhere.

Changes of this nature have, quite simply, changed the script for marketing. Regardless of whether you choose mobile marketing, social media marketing, or any other digital endeavor, rest assured you will have the opportunity to learn new things on a daily basis.

While the constant industry change provides the big-picture reason to embrace digital marketing, there are plenty of other reasons a digital marketing career may speak to you directly. For a job seeker, it is always comforting to know that the role you fill today may be valuable to different industries in the years ahead. Few employees like the feeling that they are locked into an industry for life, if only for the sole reason that their job experience becomes needlessly limiting. Recent research from the Bureau of Labor Statistics highlights that the average worker stays at their job for just 4.4. years. With that said, more than 9 in 10 millennials only plan to stay at their job for less than three years, according to the Future Workplace "Multiple Generations @ Work" survey of nearly 1,200 employees and 150 managers. If millennials make good on these plans, that means they will likely work between 15 and 20 jobs over a lifetime of employment.

Working in one of these fields will not preclude you from seeking work in an entirely separate industry. In fact, so long as you have those difficult to find digital marketing skills that will be discussed throughout this book, you will set yourself apart no matter what industry you are seeking to enter.

While the industries that are available to a digital marketing professional are vast, it is also important to note that a career in digital marketing is open to just about anyone. This is another significant perk of pursuing a digital marketing career.

You will find that digital marketing careers are not going to place a prohibitive barrier to entry when it comes to finding a job. Sure, you may need to hone a few skills, but the jobs are not going to be locked away behind a particular degree in the same way as legal or medical professions. In fact, if you are an attorney, you have the ability to join the digital marketing revolution by becoming a legal content writer or by bolstering a brand's privacy policy. Digital marketing positions are filled by people with a wide range of educational and professional backgrounds. What matters most is whether you have a passion for the job and the know-how to fulfill the role.

The quality of the job opportunities arguably surpasses the availability of digital marketing jobs. Digital marketing positions tend to offer quick career progression, which has the tangible benefit of rapid financial growth and higher salary. Digital marketing constantly demands that employees gain new skills and knowledge, which ensures employees can tout these experiences on their resume in turn. Once a digital marketer can show a proven track record based on an ability to produce for clients, earning potential increases. Such evolution based on varied marketing experience is proven by Rohit Prabhakar, the Head of Digital Marketing & Technology for McKesson.

In a wide-ranging interview for MarTechSeries, he noted that he got his start as a software engineer before putting those skills to use as a web developer, an architect, and a program manager. Eventually, he used these credentials to move into a sales role at a Fortune 500 firm before moving into product management, where he was introduced into marketing. From there, the transition was made, but the journey was a rewarding, varied ascent to heading McKesson's digital marketing efforts.

Should you nab one of the jobs that offer similarly rapid career advancement opportunities, another benefit of a digital marketing career will become apparent in short order. Digital marketing offers a variety of fulfilling opportunities, preventing a digital marketing employee from being stuck doing the same job tasks for years on end. If you ever talk to a digital marketer about their job and/or career, you will quickly learn that they do not have to be stuck in the same job function or with the same company for long. In fact, a career as a digital marketer requires you to be creative, innovative, and flexible for that very reason. An employee may find themselves working on the latest mobile app one day and video streaming an important project the next.

Even your role within a company is prone to shift in short order. For example, imagine you are working for a retail company as a product specialist, which helped you gain an appreciation of the company's target audience and market. Those skills could push you toward a promotion on the agency side of the business, participating in a targeted ad campaign based upon the crucial insight into the ad campaign's target audience gained as the product specialist. This kind of synergistic balance is typical throughout the digital marketing industry, meaning the work will be varied and the opportunities to learn are ongoing and readily available.

Digital marketing careers also provide you with the ability to choose a great work-life balance. Unlike medicine, law, and similar fields known for long hours and grinding employees down, digital marketing is capable of providing employees with a better balance between work and family, as shown by Glassdoor's recent list of the 25 best jobs for work-life balance. This list revealed that digital marketing positions fill 6 of those 25 job slots. Not only will these jobs be in high demand for the foreseeable future, they also provide opportunity for balance and flexibility needed to have a social life and spend time with those who matter most.

The reason digital marketing gives you this choice and flexibility is because the industry is already a universal one. With the rise of technology and globalization, brands have a global audience, and that means digital marketing is a truly global job market. The reality of this global marketplace is that jobs are available in both large and midsized companies. In effect, businesses of any size that understand the need for digital marketing will have meaningful job opportunities that can be the launching pad for a great career.

The notion that digital marketing is only for large corporations is an outright myth. Small businesses that use their budgets wisely achieve excellent results through digital marketing, making these companies stand out among the competition. Regardless, do not think you are limited to just local and small business jobs or jobs at large corporations and marketing firms. Since digital marketing carries such an online focus, you may be able to find excellent telecommuting job opportunities, which could result in a fulfilling digital marketing career from home. Whatever your passion and dreams of a digital marketing career might look like, there is a great chance you will find a digital marketing position to bring those dreams to fruition.

## WHY DIGITAL MARKETING IS THE CAREER PATH FOR YOU

As a digital marketer, you must stay on the cutting edge in order to succeed. Competition is simply too fierce to let stagnation or complacency infiltrate the company culture. The successful marketing personality rejects complacency at its core, which is at the root of everything you should do. The ability to think critically, plan creatively, and stay one step ahead of the competition in a continuously changing field ought to keep you excited and energized.

Digital marketers should also want to anticipate market trends, not just react to them. In many industries, a change happens and then it is up to a business to react to those changes appropriately. Of course, that happens in digital marketing as well, but the digital marketing industry's quick changes give the best marketers the chance to stay one step ahead of the changes.

If you are able to anticipate where the digital space is moving before those changes happen, your brand will enjoy a significant competitive advantage. Marketers should relish that game of cat and mouse. An old Chinese proverb once said that a wise man "adapts himself to circumstances, as water shapes itself to the vessel that contains it." Similarly, digital marketing success depends on always trying to stay at least one step ahead of the industry, not just the competition.

Digital marketing also exists as a way to connect the world in ways that improve lives. Even if you are working for a large corporation's digital marketing team, you have the chance to connect that corporation with the people whose lives are improved by the company's products.

The best digital marketers adhere to the principle of helping other businesses succeed. Whether those businesses are small or large, helping businesses achieve their dreams and visions is an incredibly rewarding experience. Helping other businesses reach their digital marketing vision should show you just how much hard work and creativity it takes to make a business succeed. When your digital marketing solutions are able to give businesses the boost they need to stand out online and in their industry, all the hard work will have been worth it. Digital marketing gives entrepreneurs like yourself the luxury of seeing the difference work makes in the lives of others each day.

## DIGITAL MARKETING IS THE CAREER FOR YOU IF YOU HAVE THE FOLLOWING FIVE CHARACTERISTICS:

* Motivation
* Willingness to Learn
* The Ability to Anticipate Trends
* The Desire to Connect to the World and Improve Lives
* The Goal to Succeed and Help Others Succeed

# 02

//////////////////////////////////////////////////

# CHOOSING ECOMMERCE AS A LAUNCHPAD TO A DIGITAL MARKETING CAREER

---

## WHAT YOU WILL LEARN IN THIS CHAPTER:

* The Future of Retail Is Online
* Why Brick and Mortar Has Gone Extinct Where Online Business Thrives
* How Beacons and Similar Technologies Are Personalizing the eCommerce Experience
* How Micro-Moments Provide Billions of Sales Opportunities for Brands Every Day
* The Common Trait All eCommerce and Internet Retail Jobs Have in Common

According to 2014 eMarketer data, eCommerce sales in the United States are expected to hit the $500 billion dollar mark by 2018. China, for their part, is expected to enjoy more than $1 trillion in eCommerce sales, and the United Kingdom is expected to reach well over $100 billion in eCommerce sales as well.

Not only is eCommerce and internet retail a rising force in terms of digital marketing employment, it is also the inevitable future for any business or corporation that plans on success in the 21st century. In 2015, the largest online retailers grew 14%, from $298.3 billion in 2014 to $341.7 billion in 2015. Store sales, by contrast, grew a mere 3% over the same timeframe. In 2016, U.S. eCommerce jumped another 15.6%, from $341.7 billion to $394.86 billion.

A recurring theme of digital marketing is that constant adaptation and improvising is critical for business success, and statistics like these reinforce that notion. ECommerce is a great digital marketing sector to jump into because businesses need to have a strong internet sales presence to succeed in the modern business environment. If you want to work in a field of digital marketing that will continue to grow as businesses increasingly transition toward a reliance on online sales, eCommerce and internet retail is an ideal fit.

In short, the way of the future is, broadly speaking, Amazon's more than it is Walmart's. If you have your doubts, that is understandable. After all, Walmart is a retail giant known the world over for offering affordable prices in its brick and mortar stores. Despite this, Amazon owns nearly 75% of the market share when it comes to total eCommerce sales. Compare that to Walmart's modest 2.8%, and it is easy to see why Walmart acquired eCommerce site Jet.com for $3 billion. Jet's eCommerce platform lets Walmart try to take on Amazon's vast online sales numbers head-on, by offering lower prices than Amazon, which has grown immensely in recent years. In effect, Walmart understands the reality of sales in the 21st century and hopes to cut into Amazon's sizeable online sales advantage.

Online shoppers have already surpassed traditional shoppers for years in certain key respects, and businesses that fail to appeal to the online shopper are setting themselves up for failure. Still, Amazon is not acting passive. It has purchased Souq.com in the Middle East, highlighting the fact that intense competition in the eCommerce space will continue to fuel growth in this field. For aspiring digital marketers, this means jobs for skilled eCommerce marketers will continue to be essential.

Notice that, in this comparison, Walmart is always reacting to the moves Amazon makes. The acquisition of Jet.com is just one such example. When Amazon created Prime Day, it generated large amounts of free publicity and customer excitement. Walmart took a "if you can't beat them, join them" approach and tried to have a large sale of their own. Similarly, Amazon has embraced the cloud and video streaming solutions to provide its Prime members with thousands of videos, streaming music, and similar perks. Walmart, in contrast, has no such incentive to entice customer loyalty. Investors have taken note of these differences, choosing to invest in Amazon far more than Walmart. In the process, Amazon has surged above $1,000 a share in 2017. One of the reasons Amazon outpaces Walmart as a growth stock is the reality that Walmart plays from behind when it comes to eCommerce and innovation.

This positive outlook for Amazon mirrors the future of internet retail, marketing, and eCommerce. Do not think that the future is solely Amazon's and the rest of the corporate giants, however. Platforms like Shopify empower individuals to run their own stores, and digital marketing is critically important for these businesses as well.

The Kewl Shop, a Shopify store selling dresses, shoes, and leggings, needed to find a way to increase their bottom line. Like most small businesses, they did not necessarily have the finances to invest heavily in better marketing. This is one of the great benefits of digital marketing, where major marketing success can be accomplished without significant expenses. Selling women's clothing is a competitive business, but the Kewl Shop used email marketing automation to differentiate itself from the competition, developing a weekly email series for customers. We will discuss the specifics of email marketing automation in the chapter on email marketing, but the takeaway here is that a small Shopify store like The Kewl Shop was able to boost its monthly revenue by 22% by using effective digital marketing tactics.

Similar success stories abound, providing optimistic financial forecasts for both small and large brands. As a result, it is unsurprising brands are working to bolster their eCommerce staff and digital marketing professionals in order to tap into these growth opportunities. Even now, large corporations have hundreds of employees working in eCommerce departments across the world to ensure their global internet retail efforts are a success. Similarly, small and midsized brands will also need to lean on skilled marketers as a driving force to help their brands grow. Not everyone will end up working for an eCommerce giant, but it will be the innovations of marketers at the small and midsized level that just might create the next Shopify and spur another eCommerce evolution.

## HOW ECOMMERCE AND INTERNET RETAIL HAS EVOLVED AND WILL CONTINUE TO THRIVE

Shopping on the web is now synonymous with 21st century living, but this was not always the case. ECommerce, a sector of digital marketing with a fascinating history worth exploring, cause this evolution. In the early 1980s, colleges and universities were the primary place you would find a computer. Home PC use had yet to become mainstream, but sending emails and sharing documents via BITNET and USENET became common across college campuses. In time, home PC users began using message boards provided by a company known as CompuServe, who introduced the Electronic Mall in 1984. This online mall allowed users to purchase goods from more than 100 online retailers, and while the service was not a financial success, it did pave the way for online retail and eCommerce today. By the time the National Science Foundation lifted its ban on commercial internet use in 1991, we were well on our way toward the eCommerce revolution brought about by eBay and Amazon.

It is one thing to recognize that eCommerce and internet retail has shifted the business landscape for good, but it is another matter entirely to understand that shift was decades in the making. Similarly, understanding how digital marketing has helped internet retail take off is key to understanding why a career in this field would be so fulfilling. In fact, the evolution of eCommerce is due in no small part to digital marketing's influence.

For proof of this, look no further than the innovations pioneered by platforms like BigCommerce, WooCommerce, and Shopify. Platforms of this nature made it possible for almost anyone to start an online storefront and run a business. This is a natural evolution of the eBay model in many respects, where it became possible to go into business for oneself rather than relying on the traditional eBay storefront model. Social networks, social media, and similar aspects of digital marketing have made it easier for these small businesses on Shopify to get their name out there and gain valuable attention for their brands. If these possibilities did not exist, it would be difficult to imagine Shopify and the latest eCommerce evolutions enjoying the successes they have had.

As brick and mortar establishments falter, digital marketing will continue to play an important role in driving eCommerce sales as many industries continue to enjoy eCommerce success. For proof of this, look no further than Blockbuster. Before Netflix, Blockbuster was the big name in video rentals. You drove to one of their brick and mortar locations to find the movies you wanted to rent, and life was good. At least, that is what consumers thought until they learned of the convenience of Netflix and their DVD subscription plans. Having movies sent directly to your mailbox made movie watching convenient and affordable. Before long, Netflix was operating as the eCommerce juggernaut we know today, with its affordable online streaming plans. All the while, Blockbuster continued trying to save its dying brick and mortar locations. By the time Blockbuster shuttered for good, it had lost $1.1 billion in revenue and was valued at a mere $24 million. Netflix, in contrast, had grown to a valuation of $13 billion. Many other eCommerce entities are following the Netflix roadmap and are transforming industries that previously relied on brick and mortar.

For example, the music industry has increasingly shifted from physical CD and album purchases to an iTunes and digital purchase business model. While there will always be those who prefer a physical album or even a vinyl record, the fact remains that streaming music now comprises more than half of the U.S. music industry. Additionally, digital music outsold physical sales for the first time in 2016, and this trend is not expected to slow in the years ahead. Businesses that continue to raise brand awareness without tapping into digital marketing's benefits are poised to be left behind just like Blockbuster or other brands focused exclusively on selling physical products.

Technology will continue to push eCommerce and all of digital marketing to continue innovating. For example, before the rise of mobile, eCommerce and internet retail thrived on desktop PCs, limiting the scope of the marketing potential. Today, the surge of mobile devices ensures that potential customers have a personalized medium for receiving eCommerce marketing regardless of location. By 2020, it is expected that there will be more than

6 billion mobile phones in use worldwide, overtaking the number of basic phone subscriptions. ECommerce and the way we market them needs to adapt to the change in consumer buying behavior as a result of technology evolution. ECommerce professionals are well aware of the fact that 41% of consumers check their mobile device multiple times every hour. In short, marketing professionals know how consumers behave, and eCommerce marketers will take the necessary actions to reach these customers. How will the industry evolve and adapt to these realities? There are a few changes to this industry a potential job seeker should expect.

First, eCommerce marketing is going to continue to shift towards a location-based approach. If you have no clue what location-based services and/or marketing is, think back to some of the apps you have used on your phone. Have you ever accepted an app's request to use your device's current location? If so, that was your way of opting in and allowing location-based services. For internet marketers, location-based marketing is poised to have a dynamic influence on how eCommerce marketing changes in the coming years. Beacon technology—low cost gadgets that help brands detect where customers are at any moment—will continue to help eCommerce marketers send relevant push notifications, promotions, and similarly helpful information to their target audience. Already, beacons are predicted to drive up to $44 billion in retail sales in 2016 alone. With data like this, expect location-based digital marketing to continue playing a large role in internet retail's marketing evolution.

Second, expect eCommerce marketing to continue focusing on personalization. Take Apple's use of beacons as a great illustration of how personalized customer interaction becomes intelligent beacon usage. Apple created their very own iBeacons and implemented them in all of their United States stores. This shift was made in December of 2013, right before the frenzied holiday shopping period. Apple cleverly combined their brick and mortar storefronts with eCommerce by using the iBeacons to provide shopper notifications when an order was assembled in the in-store stock room. This helped busy shoppers immediately know when their order was available for pickup, helping them save valuable time during the holidays. The beacons have also been used to help consumers buy products and accessories from their iPhones, view their phone's upgrade eligibility, and see local information about what is happening in Apple stores. This unique blend of traditional brick and mortar commerce and eCommerce is a great way to personalize a brand both online and offline.

ECommerce marketing typically relies on targeting buyers directly, and the most efficient way to target individuals in ways that drive sales requires personalizing the marketing approach. Personalization has long been a key driver of digital marketing success, but it is even more important for eCommerce marketers clamoring for the attention of busy consumers on their mobile devices. Seventy-three percent of consumers prefer doing business with brands that use personal information to make the shopping experience more personalized and relevant to their specific wants and needs. Retail marketing in the digital space must tap into this desire. Think of this evolution as a natural extension of living in a post-Netflix world. Consumers love having their preferences brought to their attention in a clear and easily understandable format. ECommerce teams that tap into this desire are likely to reap the benefits of taking a personalized and attentive marketing approach.

A consumer's daily life is filled with hundreds of these micro-moments each day. Imagine that you need to make a conference call, but your microphone finally breaks after three years. You need a new one immediately. This is a micro-moment. Who is going to get this business? In all likelihood, it is a company like Amazon who can offer a service like Amazon Now. By providing a service where that microphone can be delivered in two hours, Amazon just capitalized on that micro-moment in a way the competition could not. Micro-moments like these occur each and every day when consumers set their goals, solve their problems, try new things, or evaluate purchase decisions. Small businesses are just as capable of utilizing micro-moments by making mobile friendly websites and engaging in digital marketing that make their brands more easily discovered. If a small business's mobile website or app makes it easy for a consumer to make an immediate purchase as soon as the need arises, they are taking critical steps toward standing out from their competitors. Companies that understand how to tap into these opportunities are the ones that will come out on top in the eCommerce future. Understanding the needs of customers in the moment is one thing, but data must also be used and analyzed to make sure the customer's needs are satisfied in those micro-moments.

ECommerce marketing teams must take advantage of these opportunities, and many are already taking steps to do so. ECommerce retailers are already hard at work assessing how to get a consumer's attention when these moments arise. If Google's research is any indicator, demographics-based targeting is not enough. Google found that using only demographics targeting means retailers could miss out on greater than 70% of potential shoppers on a mobile device. Seizing these opportunities requires a focused assessment as to what the consumer actually wants in these given moments. For example, if an eCommerce music platform can use targeted information to determine that a mobile user loves rap music, it is easier to send relevant push notifications and alerts about some of the most exciting new hits and albums within the genre.

These are just a few of the most important changes that are likely coming for eCommerce and internet retail marketing, but they showcase the reality that these marketing efforts are an integral component of digital marketing's future.

## ECOMMERCE AND INTERNET CAREER OPPORTUNITIES

There are significant differences in company culture, size, and scope that anyone interested in this field should know. Even if you are employed within a specialty field of a large corporate department, it is likely that you will interact with other department teams and learn about their areas of eCommerce expertise tangentially. This level of opportunity and specialization provides outstanding promotional opportunities. If you need a career change in the future, work in one of these large departments is a great value add to a job application.

The story of Tobias Lutke, the founder of Shopify, is a great example of how years of work in a separate department can prepare you for success in eCommerce. In 2004, Lutke was a burnt out programmer who was tired of developing financial backend software. Lutke wanted to pursue his passion and sell snowboards, but existing eCommerce platforms were lacking. Using his extensive knowledge of backend software systems and his discovery of Ruby on Rails, Lutke built the software himself. Today, we call that software Shopify, which is the eCommerce platform powering hundreds of thousands of stores around the world. Without his programming background, Shopify may not exist as the eCommerce juggernaut we know today.

Another key benefit to consider when thinking of applying for a corporate eCommerce position is building your resume. Regarding the workload at a large enterprise, if you are a go-getter who wants to work on vast projects, few career opportunities in eCommerce will satisfy you as much as finding employment at a large company. Since you will likely be placed in a specialized role, workers who prefer a clear sense of job description in a rapidly evolving field will find many reasons to make a large company their eCommerce home.

There are plenty of reasons to choose employment with a smaller eCommerce department as well. Job seekers who want to see their work make a difference will love the appeal of working in a smaller department. Every beneficial marketing maneuver you make is likely to have a far greater effect on a small company, especially when compared to companies with billion dollar budgets. Small companies are also nimble and resourceful with respect to making quick adaptations and responses to a rapidly changing industry. There are many other benefits to working in a smaller department, such as the fact that you will be able to see how your efforts directly affect business revenue. This level of responsibility will help you learn to execute different strategies far more effectively than the typical team-based environment at larger companies.

Whether applying for employment at a large agency, a small business, or a corporation, as a prospective eCommerce digital marketing employee, you should identify the managerial structure of the company. This key information will help in determining the organizational commitment to eCommerce and digital marketing. For example, if a potential high-level job reports to someone in an "out of sight and out of mind" office, that could indicate a lack of organizational commitment to eCommerce. Alternatively, if a high-level eCommerce employee reports to the CEO, owner, president, or similarly top level personnel, it is likely that the department is properly valued. No matter whether you would prefer employment in a large or small company, do the research necessary to ensure that the marketing department you wish to work for is a top priority for the company. Otherwise, you may have higher risk of job dissatisfaction and needless roadblocks to the fulfilling digital marketing career you deserve.

If these cutting-edge eCommerce innovations and marketing tactics have piqued your interest, you should review the following promising job titles and positions available in the eCommerce and internet retail industries.

## ECOMMERCE CUSTOMER SERVICE REPRESENTATIVE

**Required Skills:**

- Ability to Handle Online Order Processing
- Maintain all Avenues of Customer Communication to Improve the Brand's Reputation
- Process Orders, Customer Service Issues and RMA Returns
- Familiarity with Shipping Policies
- Ability to Plan and Strategize to Handle and Prioritize Customer Concerns

**Expected Salary: $30,000 to $40,000**

For a brand's eCommerce efforts to succeed, there needs to be good service. If you are a looking for an entry-level job to help you climb the digital marketing ladder in this field, take a look at finding a position as an eCommerce customer service representative.

The customer service representative is tasked with handling the company's online order processing platforms, so experience with these platforms is beneficial. Just as importantly, however, the representative must also be capable of effectively communicating with customers and resolving their concerns. In the process, the brand's reputation and image is improved thanks to the work of dedicated representatives.

The customer service rep is also expected to handle customer issues via phone call and/or email, solving issues like customer returns and product questions. As such, the representative should also be familiar with shipping policies and claim procedures when issues arise due to transit and shipping problems.

The representative may need to field calls and emails from multiple customers at a time, which requires the representative to be capable of prioritizing customer concerns to effectively resolve the needs of all customers.

## ECOMMERCE ANALYST

**Required Skills**

- Proficiency with Marketing Automation Technology
- A Working Familiarity with Analytics and Database Tools
- The Ability to Suggest Actionable Improvements to the eCommerce Platform
- Set Up and Manage Listings on the Company's Online Marketplaces
- Work to Create Product Descriptions and Keywords that Will Ensure Optimum Performance

**Expected Salary: $40,000 to $55,000**

As the job title implies, the analyst's role is to analyze and oversee key aspects of the brand's online marketplaces. As such, a working familiarity with analytics, database tools, and substantive proficiency with marketing automation technology are all required.

With these abilities, the analyst is able to suggest actionable improvements to the brand's eCommerce platform. Beyond the analyst's value in providing insight, he or she must also be able to set up and manage listings on the company's online marketplace. The analyst uses data to analyze the performance of every product listing, ensuring that product descriptions and keywords on a given listing are optimized for ideal performance.

From perfecting individual listings to making key recommendations to eCommerce management, the role of a skilled analyst goes a long way toward determining the success of a brand's eCommerce department.

## ECOMMERCE MARKETING MANAGER

**Required Skills**

- Manage a Company's eCommerce Storefronts and Platforms to Meet Key Objectives and Sales Goals
- Direct and Oversee All eCommerce Products, Services and Web Content
- Develop Important Strategies for Achieving Company eCommerce Goals
- Effectively Communicate with Lower Level and Higher Level Department Professionals

- The Ability to be Self-Motivated and Motivate a Team

**Expected Salary: $70,000 to $90,000**

The eCommerce manager is tasked with managing a company's online platforms to ensure eCommerce objectives and sales goals are met. As such, the manager is expected to be capable of directing and overseeing all the products, services, and web content on eCommerce storefronts and platforms.

Perhaps most importantly, the manager must also develop plans and strategies for achieving company sales goals. Often, these plans directly rely on the insights provided by an eCommerce analyst, which is why skilled analysts are capable of working their way up the ladder to marketing manager and beyond.

The marketing manager, then, serves a key communication function within the department. The manager must be capable of discussing key matters with both lower level employees (analysts) and higher level employees (the Director of eCommerce). At all times, the manager is expected to keep the team focused and adhering to important deadlines. For this reason, the marketing manager should be not only self-motivated but also capable of motivating the team.

## DIRECTOR OF ECOMMERCE

**Required Skills**
- Handling a Large Number of the Company's Websites
- Oversee Large Volumes of Transactions Each Year
- Overseeing the Company's Online Presence
- Executing the Company Vision for eCommerce and Internet Retail
- An Established Track Record of Strategic Thinking and Long-Term Vision

**Expected Salary: $90,000 to $125,000**

The specific title for this position may vary, but ultimately, this is the position in charge of the department. Regardless, it is likely this person reports directly to the company CEO. This person is the "captain" of the company's entire online presence, serving to steer the company toward online success.

As such, few employees in the company carry as much responsibility as the eCommerce department head.

The department leader of a large company is often charged with the task of handling large numbers of branded websites that are responsible for billions of dollars in transactions each year. As such, the eCommerce head is tasked with providing the expertise, vision, and department leadership needed to effectively direct and execute the company's strategic eCommerce and internet retail plans. While eCommerce is their primary focus, these high-level executives often work in tandem with other high-level executives in crucial planning conferences that shape the company's overall vision as well.

Department heads must manage their teams to ensure that teams have the tools and resources needed to capably handle the company's online sales, design, operations, and technology needs. Given the vast degree of business knowledge and leadership skills needed, a successful department head must have years of experience, but this is not the sole criteria. This position also requires an established track record of having a long-term vision and strategic outlook. If you have aspirations to one day rise to this level within any company, start thinking with a long-term focus in the here and now. Digital marketing employees that think this way from day one are the employees that rise the ranks. They understand the big picture thinking needed to fill these types of C-level executive roles.

While this job position is far from an entry-level position, it is a career path for a young college graduate to aspire to if they choose to pursue an eCommerce career.

## VP OF ECOMMERCE

### Required Skills

- Overseeing Almost All Aspects of eCommerce
- The Ability to Cross-Function and Communicate with VPs and Executives in Other Marketing Departments
- Create Performance Standards and Goals the Department Must Reach
- Closely Monitor All Online Content and Analytics Related to eCommerce

* Track Industry Changes and Make Necessary Decisions That Keep the Brand's eCommerce Efforts Fresh and Relevant

**Expected Salary: $150,000+**

For most of the career options you will find in digital marketing, the Vice President of a given department is usually getting close to the top rung of the career ladder. If you make it to VP after years of hard work, expect to have many cross-functional aspects of your job. In other words, expect to work closely with the VP of other departments to ensure all departments are working toward one cohesive digital marketing approach.

You will still be in charge of nearly all aspects of the company's eCommerce business. This requires overseeing just about everything you can imagine involving eCommerce. The VP is responsible for oversight on business planning, content strategy, content development, web design, customer service, and web analytics.

As such, the VP should be capable of leading an entire department and working independently. It is the VP who creates performance standards, goals, and benchmarks the rest of the department must meet. All analytics and content related to eCommerce is closely monitored to ensure the brand's eCommerce vision remains fresh and relevant in light of any industry changes. When it comes to steering the eCommerce ship, the VP is the company title that has the hands on the wheel.

## ALTERNATIVE EMPLOYMENT OPTIONS

The previous job titles and descriptions focused on large and small company employment because they comprise most of the job opportunities in the field. However, when conducting a job search, do not forget about vendors that work with these small and large companies. On the large scale, you may have heard of Accenture, a company that provides eCommerce services, digital marketing, analytics, and mobility services to clients. There are plenty of smaller companies fulfilling eCommerce roles just like this for their clients. These reliable vendors have an integral part to play in eCommerce, and while they are not often discussed as potential employers in digital marketing, they are looking for qualified professionals to help them deliver results to the companies they serve.

While these are great landing spots for professionals with a firm grasp on eCommerce and internet retail, these positions are typically available to employees with years of experience in the field. These vendors utilize complex technology and talented teams of managers, developers, and digital experts to provide their services to large companies for a reason. These services are in demand by companies precisely because the level of training needed to achieve these results "in-house" is a daunting proposition.

As such, do not expect to land one of these desirable jobs without getting started at a company level first. If you have years of experience in the field, do not forget about these jobs if you are seeking a second, third, or fourth job in eCommerce. It is likely these vendors are looking for someone with your level of experience and qualifications.

## THE COMMON THREAD LINKING ALL ECOMMERCE JOBS

While this chapter has covered a wide range of different jobs, company outlooks, and organizational structures, there is one unifying link all of these job opportunities have in common. The common theme is that if you want someone to hire you in a digital marketing department because of your eCommerce expertise, you need to start participating in the industry yourself. Create a website and learn some tools of the trade firsthand. Showing that you are self-starter and a motivated job candidate will set you apart when looking for junior positions or more advanced roles. People with hiring authority in these companies want passionate employees who are creative problem solvers, and who can adjust to situations. Nothing tells a company you are prepared to do that quite like having the firsthand knowledge of trying, failing, and succeeding at various digital marketing endeavors.

Before long, you will find you landed that job you always dreamed of achieving. Once you snag that job you always wanted, the journey just begins. You will need to remain a lifelong learner who is forever curious, testing and applying the knowledge learned to various eCommerce scenarios. In that way, the knowledge learned will truly become your own, with working theories based on what has and has not worked in real-world applications.

Alternatively, understand that eCommerce success stories are filled with details of how self-starters and entrepreneurs found their own success. If you take the time to educate yourself on the industry and available opportunities, never discount the possibility of becoming an entrepreneur. Even the simplest ideas turn into remarkable stories of dedication and achievement. Take Sophia Amoruso, for example, who worked a series of odd jobs selling sandwiches at Subway and serving as an art school security guard. She haggled at thrift stores, dove into dumpsters and turned what she found into a $100 million fashion empire on her personal eBay store, Nasty Gal Vintage. She later turned these successes into a fashion empire as founder of Nasty Gal Co. and the successful autobiography #GirlBoss. Now, her journey is being told in the Netflix Original series, *Girlboss*.

If this book and other educational resources helps identify an eCommerce career at a major company or to self-start your way to your entrepreneurial empire, you should take the leap and start your journey toward a successful eCommerce career.

INTENTIONALLY LEFT BLANK

# MOBILE HAS PAVED THE WAY FOR DIGITAL MARKETING CAREER OPPORTUNITIES

## WHAT YOU WILL LEARN IN THIS CHAPTER:

* How Mobile Marketing is Uniquely Capable of Providing Personalized Marketing to Anyone, Anywhere
* How Mobile Marketing's Constant and Direct Channel Marketing Tactics Propel Digital Marketing Forward
* What Mobile Marketing Offers You in Terms of Career Choice
* Why Mobile Marketing is a Skill You Cannot Afford Not to Master
* Which Mobile Marketing Job Titles are Promising Career Paths in this Field

Simply look around at the smartphone, TV, or laptop in your home, and you will find that the evidence of technology's influence on our lives is unmistakable. A mobile device or some essential piece of technology is within arm's reach at all times. To this point, there are more than 2.6 billion smartphones in use globally, and that figure will balloon to 6.1 billion smartphones by

2020. At that point, the rise of mobile devices will have taken over the number of active fixed line phone subscriptions.

In effect, in just a few short years, 70% of the planet's population will be using a smartphone by 2020, a true benchmark of just how integral mobile devices have become. This mobile revolution is being led by millennials, as 2017 Pew Research reveals, 92% of the 18-29 demographic in the United States has a smartphone. Similarly, 88% of the 30-49 demographic has a smartphone, but these high figures sharply tail off at 74% and 42% for the 50-64 and 65+ demographics, respectively.

Given that nearly every person from a millennial age onward will have a smartphone in the future, these statistics translate to a significant growth potential in mobile marketing. While "the year of mobile" has been an idea thrown around for quite some time, it is more accurate to say that mobile's time is already here. Of course, mobile marketing's potential will only continue to grow as more smartphones come into use around the world. That figure will only increase between the time I typed these words and you, the reader, have the opportunity to read this sentence.

The key takeaway of this data is the inevitability of the fact that mobile will shape and influence every marketing job in some way. In the not too distant future, a sophisticated understanding of mobile will be a requirement for excelling in the digital marketing industry. Those who take the time to understand mobile and tap into its possibilities will thrive, and those who fail to adapt will likely be left behind. In this way, mobile marketing is a key transitional catalyst for transitioning traditional marketing into the future of digital marketing. Cindy Krum puts it succinctly in her book, *Mobile Marketing: Fin•ing Customers No Matter Where They Are*, by advising her readers that mobile marketing is "something you can't afford not to master." Highlighting the reasons why the potential for mobile marketing is so celebrated will demonstrate the truth of Krum's words.

## MOBILE MARKETING IS UNIQUELY PERSONALIZED

Mobile marketing, broadly speaking, is meant to encompass any strategy designed to appeal to potential customers with a marketing message on their mobile device. Mobile marketing, then, necessarily includes a wide range of marketing strategies and activities. For example, SMS messaging, app-based marketing, mobile search and image advertisements, location-based mobile marketing and creating a mobile app are all examples of mobile marketing solutions designed to offer a rich user experience to customers.

You likely notice that all of these different aspects of mobile marketing share one common theme. Mobile marketing is far and away the most personal form of marketing in the 21st century. Think of it this way: What other form of marketing allows a company or brand to reach its target audience when they wake up, have lunch, go out with friends, and even before they go to bed? Mobile phones are personal devices, not shared technology, such as a family computer, a television, or a landline phone. This means communication is uniquely targeted, allowing marketers to truly identify s customer's wants, desires, needs, and user interaction preferences. With this personalization comes the unique opportunity for brands to learn exactly what a specific customer wants before delivering a winning marketing message for that customer, specifically.

Imagine a large company is building a large mobile marketing campaign. The company may have a series of SMS messages, apps, and video content to deliver to their global audience. The personalization of mobile helps narrow down which mobile users are most receptive to each component of the mobile marketing campaign. This, in and of itself, is a game changer for the industry. The Starbucks app is a great example of how personalization builds brands in a positive way. The app provides free special offers and birthday gifts, loyalty programs, complimentary beverages, special discounts, and messaging that is personalized based on customer responses to Starbucks surveys. While these are great touches, Starbucks was not content to leave personalization to chance. They also updated its app to allow playlist viewability. In essence, this means that when a customer hears a great song at a physical Starbucks location, they can save the song they just heard to a playlist within the app. Users then access that playlist through Spotify after leaving the store and going about their day.

There are a few reasons why this approach worked so well. First, Starbucks inherently knew from their company data that 21% of Starbucks transactions are completed via their mobile app. Given that 11 million Starbucks customers were currently signed up for the mobile application, there was a large target audience to reach. It all came down to personalizing and engaging that audience in a meaningful way.

Free drinks, better values, quality customer loyalty programs, and having special days like your birthday valued and remembered all make a customer feel valued. Building on these personalized elements has now made Starbucks a far more relatable brand than they would have been without their mobile app. Even music is not left to chance, thanks to the innovative use of Spotify. Simply put, customers now equate Starbucks with being a personalized and essential part of their daily routine. Mobile marketing has made Starbucks the premier coffee shop for branding and personalization.

## MOBILE MARKETING IS ACTIONABLE

Mobile marketing has opened up the possibility of making a marketing message interactive and actionable in ways that were simply not possible previously. Because of technological limitations, unnecessary barriers were put in front of the marketing message and consumers, making it more difficult to respond to marketing efforts or a brand's call to action.

Take, for example, a webpage you come across with a product that interests you. Before mobile technology, you would need to browse over to the "Contact Us" page, write down the number, go to your landline, and make the phone call. The rise of mobile has eliminated those unnecessary steps, allowing you to simply click on the phone number link on your smartphone the moment you want to take action based on what you saw online. Mobile marketing, then, is all about simplification. Specifically, it is about simplifying how brands and customers interact. With easier and more effortless interaction, both customers and marketers benefit since communication is a more transparent and direct activity.

Take for example the story of how a global brand like McDonald's took advantage of mobile's actionable nature. McDonald's wanted to take advantage of so-called "night owls" who wanted to pick up some fast food after midnight. This makes sense, given that McDonald's had recently extended the hours of operation to 24 hours at many of their restaurant locations. McDonald's knew they had a great sales opportunity on which to capitalize, and they used mobile marketing to raise awareness and get foot traffic in the early morning hours.

McDonald's knew intuitively that people who are active after 11 PM are creatures of habit, whether they are working or are simply out with friends having fun. McDonald's wanted to interrupt those late-night habits with time and location specific mobile marketing that would direct their audience to a 24-hour McDonald's location.

To achieve these goals, McDonald's created a "restaurant finder" smartphone application that helped people find the closest 24-hour McDonald's. Then, with the app serving as the central hub of the marketing effort, McDonald's used social media with time-of-day targeting to drive "night owl" readers to their stores. In this way, the combination of a strong app and time-of-day and location-based mobile marketing provided actionable insight that gave a wide audience the desire to eat at McDonald's, as well as the information needed to have the desire met.

Unsurprisingly, the campaign greatly contributed to McDonald's sales efforts. The chain experienced a 4% overnight sales value growth and a generous ROI. The lesson of this case study is that a mobile-led campaign that uses effective targeting to a specific audience translates to an actionable message that drives sales.

## MOBILE EMPOWERS BRANDS TO SPEAK WITH AN AUDIENCE DIRECTLY

College students and young professionals are always on the go, and so is mobile marketing. If portability and constant connectedness to your world appeals to you, then the nature of mobile as a direct marketing channel is a perfect match. Before mobile devices became the norm for billions of people, computers were the most efficient way to communicate. Whether you were in class, on a date, or hanging out with friends, there was no real way to reach you until you were back at your computer. Thanks to mobile email and texting, you can always be reached, so long as your phone still has enough battery life. Even if you are occupied at a meeting or are watching a movie at the theater, your phone can receive those messages and make them available for viewing as soon as you check your phone again.

Now, effective mobile marketing can contact target users without interrupting their day. This is a significant benefit for brands worried about annoying their customers. There is a reason telemarketers are still so unpopular. Their phone calls interrupt family dinner (telemarketers are America's "most hated dinnertime interruption" for a reason), date night, or binge watching the latest season of your favorite show on Netflix. Message recipients now have the chance to view the message when it is easy or convenient for them to do so. In this way, target users have a more natural marketing experience that is more readily accepted from the start. This, in turn, allows mobile marketing the benefit of constant persistence in a way traditional marketing never could.

What do I mean by constant persistence? Well, let us rewind for a moment back to the telemarketing example. If a telemarketer interrupts family dinner, the telemarketer just might be subjected to an angry rant, followed by an angry "Take me off your call list!" Even if a telemarketer tries again, the relationship has been soured for good. In all likelihood, any future marketing efforts will go unrewarded.

Instead of needing to find out where somebody is or whether you are calling at a good time, mobile campaigns allow you to reach exactly who you need to reach when you need to market to them directly. Traditional marketing cannot even ensure the right person is reached since a home address or home phone number is tied to a location. If you want to reach the mother of the household, for example, the father may answer the phone instead. Since mobile is tied to people, not locations, you reach them directly every time. Plenty of case studies reveal how businesses use the portability and persistence of direct mobile marketing to their advantage. The ways Nike uses mobile marketing serve as excellent examples of how direct mobile marketing is implemented in an effective mobile marketing campaign.

Nike is a brand that has shown itself to be uniquely aware of the direct marketing potential of mobile. For proof of this, one need look no further than the company's Nike Grid campaign. Long before Pokemon GO took the mobile gaming world by storm with its location-based mobile gaming experience, Nike turned all of London into a giant virtual gameboard for athletes and runners. Speaking directly to its active mobile audience, Nike challenged runners to reach various checkpoints around the city, earning points wherever they ran. What transpired was a citywide competition among the London running community. Nike went on to offer badges for speed, endurance, and stamina achievements. This campaign was significant because it was Nike's first real attempt at merging real world sport performance with the brand's digital and social marketing efforts, and the attempt worked. London runners logged more than 30,000 runs that translated to a combined distance that equaled running halfway around the world.

Just two years later, Nike pioneered yet another London mobile marketing success. This time, Nike wanted to speak directly to its audience. In 2012, however, the Olympics were being held in London. Nike knew that Londoners who were watching the Olympics were more likely to be active individuals, and Nike wanted to communicate with them directly. To do this, Nike created the "#findgreatness" campaign on Twitter. Nike directly increased its visibility during the Olympics on their social media channels, and as a result, more than 16,000 tweets directly associated Nike with the word Olympics between July 27th and August 2nd of 2012. Even better, the brand gained 166,718 new Facebook fans over the course of the games. This is the power of using mobile to speak to your audience directly.

## MOBILE MARKETING IS FOR ANY BUSINESS

A key benefit of mobile marketing is that any business can tap into the successes made possible by mobile marketing, even if they are a small business. Tools are available online that can help anyone make a successful app or launch a mobile campaign. If a small business is looking to launch a full-scale mobile marketing campaign, solutions like AT&T's mobile marketing services help businesses affordably launch targeted campaigns via text message and instant messaging. If a small business needs to refine their app, solutions like Urban Airship help the brand effectively automate how push notifications and in-app messages are sent to customers.

The point is, no matter what a small business is looking to do with mobile marketing, there is an effective solution out there. To underscore this point, Nimnicht Family Dealerships showed how small business auto dealers can run a successful campaign.

This case study highlights the value of getting local customers to opt-into a small business's marketing effort. Opting in necessarily requires a customer to take extra steps that show they trust your business to not spam them, and small businesses need to reward this leap of faith.

Nimnicht Family Dealerships understood this all too well, so they chose to run a mobile marketing campaign focused on offering their mobile customers exclusive benefits. The dealership advertised they would raffle away a new car to all their mobile customers, which earned them 4,000 new opt-ins via mobile. The dealership then wisely leveraged these opt-ins by starting a promotional campaign via mobile that targeted customers looking to buy a new or used car. Combined, 9.25% of the 4,000 opt-ins were considered workable leads, meaning almost 1 in 10 of the opt-ins could lead to a new purchase.

Consider that all this took was giving away one car and providing customers with a true incentive to become a mobile customer who connected to the dealership in a new and exciting way. The lesson here is that small businesses need to differentiate themselves by providing value, whether that is through a text-to-win campaign or a leading mobile app. Regardless, mobile marketing is a key component for helping small business brands do just that.

## MOBILE MARKETING OFFERS IMMEDIACY FOR BRANDS AND CONSUMERS ALIKE

If there is one thing brands and their consumers have in common, it is that they want immediate results. For the brand, seeing immediate results is a significant benefit to their bottom line, and many consumers have been proven to be impatient when there is a product they demand. Mobile marketing lets brands target those impulse shoppers to excellent effect. Most research on impulse shopping has shown that the central factor in an impulse purchase is not any specific tactic implemented by the retailer. Rather, it is whether the shopper in question is impulsive.

In this way, eCommerce has an important advantage over brick and mortar stores since traditional storefronts lack the means to control who comes into their store to shop. Online retailers, however, when planning digital marketing campaigns, do have the opportunity to control who they provide impulse buy advertising, and since mobile is uniquely personal in nature, combining this marketing with a company's "big data" offers a unique opportunity to provide immediate results to both impulse shoppers and businesses alike.

This level of buying immediacy is far from the only immediate aspect of mobile marketing. Since mobile phones are with the user at all times (or, nearly all times), any message received on the phone becomes immediately available to the user. The best part of this form of immediacy, from a marketing perspective, is the fact that mobile users check their devices often. In fact, the average person touches their phone a staggering 2,617 times a day, according to a 2016 study conducted by Dscout. Collectively, Americans check their smartphones more than 8 billion times per day. In other words, people are only becoming more reliant on their smartphones.

Take note of the fact that these are only averages. According to a Deloitte study, younger users between the ages of 18 and 24 checked their phone an average of 74 times per day. There is great opportunity for all marketing to reach all demographics, but there is an especially unique opportunity for brands that resonate with younger audiences. Of course, this younger generation will be around for many decades to come, highlighting why mobile marketing's potential will translate to long-term and stable career opportunities.

Of course, with these marketing opportunities comes a unique challenge as well. The mere fact that mobile users check their devices many times a day does not mean a brand's message will reach the intended user easily. After all, a mobile user is checking email, texting, playing mobile games, and engaging with quality apps. In other words, only quality mobile marketing will reap the benefits of mobile marketing's immediacy potential. For this reason, mobile marketing careers are likely best suited for intermediate to advanced digital marketers with years of quality experience.

A great example of this potential comes by way of IKEA's mobile app. Furniture shopping, especially online, is a drab and boring experience. Just browse online at the typical furniture store, and you will find it is a dry and functional experience at best. It certainly is not memorable. IKEA utilized the capability of mobile marketing to drive excitement about furniture. How they did this was simple and ingenious. IKEA created a mobile app that effectively transformed its entire catalog into an interactive platform. The app let users virtually place popular IKEA products into their own living room using input from the user's smartphone camera. Then, the product was overlayed into the camera application, allowing users to visualize how an IKEA product would look in their own living space. This is the level of excitement and immediacy mobile marketing provides, and it is not surprising that IKEA's creative furniture app enjoyed well over 6 million installs. Sometimes, clever mobile marketing focused on immediacy and engagement simply needs to let the customer have fun to make sure customers engage with the brand repeatedly.

## THE COMPETITIVE NATURE OF MOBILE MARKETING

The competitive nature of mobile marketing demands a company's best marketers, and for this reason, it is likely that mobile marketing positions are not the best launching point into a digital marketing career. Still, learning valuable mobile marketing skills will make you a more desirable hire in almost any area of digital marketing since, as discussed, mobile marketing's influence will touch almost every aspect of digital marketing in the years ahead. If your previous employment gave you extensive knowledge of mobile advertising and mobile content, it is possible that you may have the ability to enter into this increasingly competitive field without other digital marketing experience.

Mobile marketing is a very measurable field, meaning experiences with things like search engine marketing, search engine optimization, paid search, and similar skills are often a prerequisite for the job. Even though most mobile marketing lets users opt-in—meaning users must choose to accept notifications from a brand—companies must still take a careful and skilled approach to avoid annoying users, which may lead them to get frustrated and unsubscribe. As such, many employers want to see that a mobile marketing job applicant has experience that demonstrates know how to remain sensitive to a mobile user's interests and preferences. In this way, getting a job in mobile marketing depends on a job applicant's understanding of the artistry of appealing to mobile users, not just the applicant's practical industry knowledge.

As such, those getting their start in the industry would be wise to focus their initial job search on digital marketing positions that give an employee insight into appealing to the desires and preferences of users. With most digital marketing positions, the technical knowledge can be learned, but not all digital marketing positions will offer the experience needed to understand the art form of creating innovative and engaging mobile campaigns. With that said, here are some of the job titles available in the mobile marketing area for intermediate and advanced digital marketing professionals.

## MOBILE MARKETING COORDINATOR

### Required Skills

- Coordinate all Mobile-Related Marketing Efforts a Company Uses
- A Keen Eye for Noticing the Trends and Levers that Will Improve a Company's Mobile Marketing Results
- The Ability to Understand What a Mobile User Wants in an App, Text Campaign or Push Notification
- Know How to Monetize Mobile Products and Work with Important Marketing Tools Related to Customer Resource Management
- Troubleshoot and Fix Issues that Negatively Affect Mobile Marketing Performance

### Expected Salary: $45,000 to $55,000

The mobile marketing coordinator needs to have a keen eye for detail, helping coordinate the brand's mobile efforts whether those efforts are a mobile app, a mobile website, or text notifications. No matter the marketing method or channel, the coordinator needs to understand the key levers that drive mobile marketing results.

To this end, knowing what users want is a critical component of coordinating effectively. Text campaigns, effective push notifications or eminently usable mobile apps all require giving end users what they need. Offer a boring or ineffective text or app, and users will quickly look elsewhere.

The coordinator's eye for detail is used to help set up the mobile campaigns to help the brand succeed. This entry-level role provides outstanding hands-on experience that helps a young professional see precisely how an effective marketing campaign must be executed.

Coordinators learn valuable tools related to customer resource management and how to monetize mobile products for improved mobile marketing results. Finally, the mobile coordinator must also learn to test and troubleshoot various mobile issues that are negatively affecting an app or text campaign's performance.

## MOBILE MARKETING ANALYST

**Required Skills**

- Support and Execute Mobile Growth Strategies
- Understand the Technical Ecosystem that Supports a Quality Mobile Marketing Effort
- Conduct Daily Reports Related to KPIs and User Retention
- Ensure App Features Run to Expectations
- Monitor App Upgrades and Campaign Strategies to Ensure Timelines are Met

**Expected Salary: $50,000 to $65,000**

The mobile analyst knows and understands the technical ecosystem underpinning the brand's mobile marketing effort. This requires both an analytical knowledge and a technical understanding of the brand's mobile solutions, particularly if apps are part of the company marketing efforts. Technical savvy is needed to ensure app features run to expectations and can be fixed if the app is not working as needed.

Beyond these technical specifications, an analyst is also tasked with supporting and executing a wide range of mobile growth strategies. For example, if a text campaign is to be launched a week after the app's release, the analyst will monitor these timelines and company strategies to keep marketing goals and timelines on schedule.

This responsibility especially extends to app upgrade cycles, which are often needed to keep an app relevant to retain users. While monitoring such activity, the analyst will also conduct daily reports that track whether key performance indicators are being met as well as whether user acquisition and retention goals are being met.

## MOBILE MARKETING MANAGER

### Required Skills

- Take a Leading Management Role in Nearly Every Aspect of a Mobile Marketing Campaign
- Use Rich Data to Make Mobile Marketing Both Interactive and Uniquely Appealing
- Analyze the Latest Data and Trends to Identify Further Marketing Opportunities or Areas of Improvement
- Use Data Trends to Identify Future Brand Opportunities
- Work Closely with Other Marketing Executives to Ensure the Brand's Marketing is Consistent

### Expected Salary: $80,000 to $90,000

The mobile marketing manager is at the middle level of the food chain with regards to an organization's mobile marketing efforts. A mobile marketing manager is expected to lead every major aspect of a mobile marketing campaign. Campaign ideas and implementation are carried out only with the mobile marketing manager's approval, and even the design and execution phases are overseen by this job role.

If you aspire to land this title, know that what starts as a simple marketing internship in college often translates into a career of climbing to the top of the mobile marketing ladder. Such was the case for Leslie Albertson, a successful mobile marketing manager for a popular iOS and Android photobook app. Leslie began her digital marketing journey as a Sr. Marketing Analyst before working her way up to Sr. Mobile Marketing Manager and, eventually, Director of Marketing. No matter how you work your way toward this position, it is important to understand that this position is for professionals who embrace the pressure of a department's success resting on your capable shoulders.

Mobile marketing managers carry significant weight in the department and are tasked with putting the right tools in place to effectively analyze a mobile campaign's results. Using big data and measurable analytics, the manager can then implement the needed changes to yield even greater returns on investment in future mobile marketing campaigns. Additionally, the mobile marketing manager also constantly seeks out the latest market research and key data trends to identify further marketing opportunities for the organization.

If you found yourself inspired by the IKEA case study referred to previously, consider that a reason to aspire to this job title. The mobile marketing manager works closely with rich media professionals in the organization. Rich media, for reference, is display advertising that uses very sophisticated technology designed to make advertisements as interactive and expertly designed as possible. The possibilities of expertly designed, interactive media are too tempting for modern digital agencies to ignore, and it is the mobile marketing manager who oversees these cutting-edge innovations.

## DIRECTOR OF MOBILE MARKETING

**Required Skills**

- Take Responsibility for the Entirety of a Department's Operations
- Frequent Communication with the Manager to Make on the Fly Adjustments to a Campaign as Needed
- Guide the Department's App Developments, Updates and Maintenance
- Improve Future Campaigns Based on Department Feedback and an Analysis of the Data
- Create Department Forecasts for Future Mobile Marketing Activities

**Expected Salary: $100,000 to $115,000**

As the head of a mobile marketing department, the director has even more responsibility than the manager. Managers tend to report directly to the Director of Mobile Marketing, making this one of the last stops up the mobile marketing ladder. Such was the case for the aforementioned Leslie Albertson.

The director is typically tasked with the entirety of the department's operations. This means all mobile apps, text campaigns, and more fall under his or her responsibility. This level of responsibility means the director communicates frequently with manager(s) to get frequent updates on the success of a campaign. This daily collaboration lets the director make important decisions and adjust campaigns on the fly when needed. Once a campaign has concluded, the director must take all feedback and implement it to improve future campaigns.

Finally, the director also works with other department directors and executives to keep the company's overall marketing strategy cohesive and unified. This typically requires coming up with a department forecast to provide a prediction for the mobile business that can help the company budget for future marketing activities and campaigns, accordingly.

## VP OF PRODUCT DEVELOPMENT

**Required Skills**

- Lead, Develop, and Inspire the Best in Tech Talent to Produce High-Quality Results Across Each Stage of the Product Lifecycle
- Create Apps and Other Innovative Mobile Products for the Brand's Marketing Effort
- Product Must Be Developed According to Plans and Details Outlined by the VP's Roadmap
- Oversee the Developments of All Products at Every Phase
- Continue to Monitor Product Performance Post-Launch to Provide Critical Support and Updates

**Expected Salary: $140,000+**

Once you have climbed to the top of the mobile marketing ladder, there are still more career titles worth aspiring toward. If you make it to Director of Mobile Marketing, the next career progression tends to be VP of Product Development.

This position comes with significant responsibility since all mobile development is helmed by the VP, who must create apps and other innovative mobile solutions that help the brand resonate with their customers. Nearly every skill mastered on the way up the ladder is relevant in a position of this scope and scale.

The VP must consider the budget of the department, the fine details of the mobile products themselves, and whether the teams are operating effectively. Most importantly, however, the VP must develop and build a roadmap from start to finish for the mobile products. This includes setting timelines from the idea phase to product development and launch. Every phase is carefully guided by the steady hand of the VP until the product is ready to be deployed and released as part of the company's marketing efforts.

Once the product has launched, the VP must then continue to monitor the app's performance to make sure the products have the proper support and updates post-launch. The job, quite simply, is the culmination of many tools learned after years of proven success in mobile marketing.

## THE UNIQUE, PERSONAL NATURE OF YOUR CAREER IN MOBILE MARKETING

The importance of mobile marketing and, subsequently, careers in this field cannot be overstated. That said, there are unique aspects of a career in mobile marketing that are worth mentioning. Every mobile user is unique, and this reality serves as the foundation of every aspect of mobile marketing. As such, it is no surprise that there are unique elements of a career in mobile marketing found nowhere else in the digital marketing field.

Careful consideration of opt-in advertising, weighing the balance of users' privacy and their desires, and the challenge of competing for the user attention all contribute to why work in this field is so special. Beyond the uniqueness of the job description and the job itself, this field also attracts a unique digital marketing personality. To explain this in further detail, imagine you are at a party. At any party, you have the chance to mingle and meet people who you do not know. In this way, getting along with people at a party is effectively marketing yourself and your personality to strangers. There are right and wrong ways to go about how you interact with others at a party, and the same is true of how you behave as a mobile marketer.

One wrong way to interact as a mobile marketing professional is being too self-centered. A self-centered person or brand is not engaged in a dialog with the listener. Put another way, he or she is just lecturing instead of listening. That does not engage people and draw them into the discussion. It pushes them away. As a mobile marketer, avoid pushing your narrative on the end user. Instead, treat mobile marketing as an open dialog where you truly listen to what your end users and customers want.

Another mobile marketing persona to avoid is the erratic persona. This is the scatterbrained marketer who throws 10 different marketing strategies at the wall to see what sticks. Customers have a hard time understanding the marketing message, as it rarely remains on topic. In the mobile marketing world, this will confuse your targeted mobile users, ensuring they will go elsewhere to find a more compelling mobile experience. Instead, a successful mobile marketer will take the time to analyze data and find out exactly what an end user wants and needs. Then, the mobile marketer will deliver that message consistently, reliably, and patiently. The consistency of this branding will lead to results.

Finally, too many brands engage in marketing that makes their brand annoying and/or obnoxious. In mobile marketing, this translates to bad timing, obnoxious push notifications, or letting knowledge of industry trends lapse so you are delivering knowledge that is out of date. Customers will not interact with brands that are irrelevant and annoying. This is why mobile marketers must constantly educate themselves and stay up to date on industry trends. Otherwise, mobile marketers and their brands run the risk of being ignored by their target audience. Once this happens, it is very difficult to undo the damage and get those customers interested in the brand once again.

I am frequently inspired by the words and work of visionaries like Seth Godin, Gary Vaynerchuk, and Avinash Kaushik. These industry luminaries have a way of translating the excitement of digital marketing in a personal and easily digestible way that makes people excited to think about the possibilities of this industry.

That is what mobile marketing is all about, and it is my hope you take this inspiration and run with it toward an exciting and intensely personal mobile marketing career. If you choose to do so, I have no doubt that you will achieve the lofty goals you set for yourself with hard work and dedication. This chapter provides you with the information and resources needed to carve your own path toward a successful mobile marketing career that fits within your vision. In the words of the great NFL coach Vince Lombardi, a person can be "as great as he wants to be. If you believe in yourself and have the courage, the determination, the dedication, the competitive drive and if you are willing to sacrifice the little things in life and pay the price for the things that are worthwhile, it can be done."

Keeping these words of inspiration in mind, dedicate yourself to the goal of a mobile marketing career, and you will amaze yourself years from now, when you look back on the progress you made over the course of your mobile marketing career.

INTENTIONALLY LEFT BLANK

//////////////////////////////////////////////////

# SOCIAL MEDIA STANDS TO PLAY A LARGE ROLE IN DIGITAL MARKETING'S FUTURE

## WHAT YOU WILL LEARN IN THIS CHAPTER:

* How Social Media Changed the Marketing Industry for Good
* Why Customers Prefer Engaging with a Social Media Brand and How Brands Can Capitalize on this Desire
* Key Lessons from the Infamous "Dell Hell" Social Media Marketing Failure and Recovery
* What it Takes to Achieve Your Social Marketing Goals
* Personalizing Your Path Toward a Successful Social Media Career

On a daily basis, in all likelihood you habitually check your Snapchat and Instagram accounts, in addition to checking for status updates and messages on Facebook. This is the power of social media, and working in this field gives you the opportunity to affect how ordinary people interact with digital technology and their world on a regular basis.

Imagine changing the world from the relative discomfort of your college dorm room, and then you could understand the possibility of social media marketing. If you have seen the critically acclaimed film *The Social Network*, then you already know social media owes much of its success to these humble beginnings. When Mark Zuckerberg first started Facebook in his early years at Harvard, even he could not have known how big social media would become in the years ahead.

Mark Zuckerberg, Facebook CEO and one of its initial founders, has even admitted that much of Facebook's success was all about timing. Facebook's humble beginnings began as thefacebook.com, a creation of Mark Zuckerberg and his college roommates at Harvard. Initially, the social media service was designed for the exclusive use of Harvard students, but it quickly expanded to include the larger Boston area. From there, the rest is history. The service rapidly expanded to become a global phenomenon valued at more than $350 billion. Now, to be sure, social media websites such as Myspace existed long before Facebook, but the likes of Facebook and Twitter pushed the social media industry forward exponentially.

On the business side, LinkedIn is another great example of social media's power to influence and shape the world. Designed as a business-focused social network by serial entrepreneur Reid Hoffman, LinkedIn was founded in 2002. Growth was slow going at first, but eventually, Hoffman achieved his vision of turning LinkedIn into an all-encompassing business social network success story.

In digital marketing, like life, successful careers in certain fields depend on good timing. A digital marketing career 10 years ago would have been much harder to come by, if only because demand for social media skills were not nearly as necessary for companies trying to reach customers online. Today, being social media savvy is a great way to have a long and fulfilling career in this industry.

## WHY CUSTOMERS PREFER ENGAGING WITH A SOCIAL BRAND

Statistics and research consistently reveal that brands that interact on social media create more meaningful customer relationships. Inbound marketing leader HubSpot asked 569 customers what amount of social media activity and visibility they expected of any given brand in 2014. Ninety-five percent of Millennials expect a brand to be active on Facebook, and 70% of the 45 to 60 year-old demographic believes a brand should have a Facebook page at the very least. The majority of customers today also expect brands to be active on at least three to four social channels.

When customers are expecting this of companies, brands and digital marketing agencies cannot afford to ignore this expectation. To do so would be to needlessly sabotage a brand's marketing capability and success. In practical terms, this means greatly increasing the chances of business failure. The drive to social media is about more than just the immediacy of fulfilling expectations, however. It is also about building long-term trust. The latest study based on consumer trust and recommendations is a 2015 Nielsen study that found 83% of people trust recommendations from peers over advertising. In fact, this figure was nearly twice as much trust compared to more traditional forms of advertising. Smart businesses understand that one of the great benefits of having a proven social media presence is that customers will come to feel like they know your brand. In the process, they will have more trust in the company and its products.

The globally renowned social media platforms Facebook, YouTube, LinkedIn, Twitter, Instagram, and similar large social media presences employ tens of thousands of social media professionals. Add up all the worldwide social media marketing opportunities at corporations, digital agencies, and small businesses, and you are looking at millions of career opportunities. Getting one of these jobs and turning it into a career requires knowing what it takes to succeed and achieve your goals.

## FROM "DELL HELL" TO A SOCIAL MEDIA SAVVY BRAND

The initial blog post written by Jarvis had a simple headline: "Dell lies. Dell sucks." By his own admission, even back in 2005, Jarvis had a so-called method to his madness. He knew that a brand's name followed by the word "sucks" was a quick way to get a snapshot of the company's ill will with consumers. He wanted to make a test to determine whether Dell read these blogs and cared enough about their customers to remedy the situation. Jarvis typed away, and before long, his blog was widely available online.

This may stun a 2016 reader, but the fact is Dell did see his blog post. They just did not care all that much. Despite the fact Jarvis's rant went viral, Dell executives seemed to believe an angry internet blogger could not harm them. How wrong they were. Other disappointed and angry customers soon joined Jarvis in sharing their awful customer service stories with Dell, which led to a devastating New York Times piece criticizing the company. Shortly thereafter, plenty of other news outlets were picking up on the scoop, interviewing angry customers, and trying to get in touch with Dell executives for comment.

Surprisingly, these angry voices in unison managed to create a PR crisis that harmed Dell's stock. The first lesson of this interaction is that when brands ignore social media, they are essentially ignoring the lifeblood of their business. Consumers who are ignored have unprecedented power today. The "Dell Hell" story is child's play compared to the importance of social media relations today. Ignore your customers, and your brand is in peril. It is as simple as that. However, that is just one lesson to be learned from Dell's story.

The second lesson serves as a reminder on what companies should do when their social media marketing efforts are not striking the right notes with a target audience. Of course, the story did not end with Dell simply not responding to this outcry. Instead, the company took steps to remedy the situation and heal the rift between the company and its customers. Instead of mourning the loss, Dell worked the situation to their advantage. After discovering this newfound potential of social media and the internet, Dell poured millions into overhauling its customer service relations. The company launched a social media program, putting thousands of employees through training programs to have better interactions with customers. From this point, Dell continued listening to customers and truly valuing their input. In the process, Dell undid much of the negativity from "Dell Hell" and turned it into a positive with improved social media branding and customer care.

## SKILLS NEEDED TO ACHIEVE YOUR GOALS IN SOCIAL MEDIA MARKETING

If you have yet to embrace social media, but are intrigued by what you have read, know that there is plenty of time to get up to speed with the latest social media developments. There are free courses and blogs available that will give you the education needed to make the most out of a career in this field. However, it is critical that you truly embrace these opportunities with passion and committed resolve. When you are passionate about your job, success follows. Here are some of the skills you will need.

## A WORKING FAMILIARITY WITH SOCIAL MEDIA MARKETING FROM A BROADENED PERSPECTIVE

Even if you do not want to pursue a digital marketing career focused on social media, it is still helpful to gain a working familiarity with social media marketing. Digital marketing fields often overlap, making knowledge in one field of digital marketing directly transferable to another. As such, even if social media is not your favorite field of digital marketing, it is still essential that you learn how to wield the influence of social media creatively and effectively.

## THE ABILITY TO FEED OFF CREATIVITY THAT CAN CREATE CONVERSATION

Know that if you feed off creative energy, social media marketing is a great path. Not only does social media marketing demand creativity, it demands a unique form of creativity designed to create conversation. So much in life is a dialog, and social media marketing is uniquely positioned to shape how that conversation takes place. Learning the latest conversation trends and what a target audience wants to talk about is an invaluable skill to have in this field. Best of all, this skill is obtained simply by being active and getting involved in the conversation. Whether those conversations take place on YouTube, Facebook, or Twitter, shaping the conversation in a meaningful way is a great way to get your start in social media marketing.

# TAKE THE TIME TO OBSERVE AND LEARN FROM THE BEST

Take the time to follow social media influencers you find interesting and observe how they interact. You will notice they take time to listen, a must for any conversation to be meaningful. Influencers are also focused, adding value to the conversation. Additionally, influencers are accessible, and it is rare that a week goes by without plenty of meaningful and thoughtful posts/ online interactions. Emulate these influencers, and you will be well on your way toward a successful social media career of your own, no matter where your digital marketing journey takes you.

Sometimes the best way to know what skills you need to succeed is to simply look at who has succeeded in your preferred marketing niche. Mel Welsh has built a career on succeeding in social media, helping Pearson increase their social media engagement by 68% while employed there. Mel then transitioned to a position at Comcast, where she managed the company's social media pages.

According to Mel, social media marketing depends on effective communication between brands and their audience. To this end, she also sees an incredible opportunity for providing better customer service via social media marketing efforts. Comcast, for example, provides a dedicated service department designed to address tweets on social media. The aspiring social media marketer would be wise to take note of these trends. A marketer who understands the importance of communication will stand out in this field.

Welsh also notes that her favorite aspect of digital marketing is the analytics aspect, which may, at first glance, come across as strange coming from a digital marketer in social media. It actually makes sense, however, since social media marketing success hinges on using social media analytics tools to learn more about an audience in order to better connect with them. The social media marketers should familiarize themselves with these tools in order to maximize their ability to connect with a target audience in an authentic and meaningful way. By mastering these tools, the aspiring marketer will make strides toward a successful career in social media.

# CAREER OPPORTUNITIES IN SOCIAL MEDIA

There are so many ways to get a start in social media that it can be difficult to know where to begin. Here are just a few ways to start browsing options and opportunities available to a new or recent graduate in social media-focused marketing.

If you plan on going a traditional route, take the time to start slow and learn the industry. Slow and steady wins the race, as they say, so do not try to cram and obtain everything there is to know about social media marketing. This leads to burnout and, worse, the inability to retain what you have "learned." Instead, take the learning process seriously and get a firm grasp on each aspect of social media marketing before moving on to a new learning topic. Every social media network has a beginning learning curve, but none of the learning curves are very steep if you put in the time. Learn the features of each network through educational resources and hands-on training workshops to learn how to better wield these networks for your marketing, as either an entrepreneur or an employee at an agency.

Finally, take the time to look at job listings in social media marketing to see how the industry is evolving. Five years from now, the digital marketing world will look very different than it does today. Staying up to date on what employers expect is a great way to take proactive efforts to obtain the skills needed to be a good fit in the industry.

If you have aspirations to make it to the top of this field as a social media manager, start learning and growing your copywriting skills, as this plays a major role in content marketing on social media platforms. Similarly, it is in your best interests to hone your design skills, which entails learning how to create images for captions and creating valuable social media posts. Most of all, all marketing via social media should help the brand communicate authentically with a genuine voice. Learning how to do this professionally at all times is an asset that will serve you well when advancing through the ranks in a social media department.

Digital marketing experts and professionals know and understand how critical social media is to a brand's success. Surprisingly, we need to remind brands of social media's importance from time to time. This is startling given the proof that businesses endanger their growth as brands by neglecting the growth opportunities of social media. The reticence of brands to embrace social media marketing represents a staggering disconnect from what digital marketing pros know and what brands think they know.

The companies and social media marketers that thrive are the ones who recognize digital marketing is a rapidly changing landscape that will always need proven social media marketing solutions. By constantly educating yourself on the latest social media happenings, you will remain on the cutting edge of the industry no matter how you choose to make a name for yourself in this field.

## SOCIAL MEDIA COMMUNITY MANAGER

**Required Skills**
- Manage the Human Element of Interacting with Customers
- Effective Communication Skills That Ensure Brand and Customer Conversations Go Smoothly
- Serving as the Voice of the Company and Customer Alike
- Taking the Steps Needed to Ensure an Online Community Thrives
- Remain Authentic and Active, Boosting a Brand's Authenticity and Awareness in the Process

**Expected Salary: $35,000 to $50,000**

The social media marketing manager is in charge of the entire social media campaign side of things, but it is the online community manager who manages the human element of interacting with customers. Namely, this manager ensures conversations with customers go smoothly and benefit the brand. As you might imagine, this requires the community manager to juggle and wear two different hats. A community manager acts as the customer's voice within the organization, taking steps to inform C-level professionals that customers were/are angry. While this is an important function, these professionals also provide the voice of the brand, especially when it is needed to calm customers or strengthen a customer's view of the brand.

This relatively recent social media position requires a manager to ensure that online communities thrive when interacting with the brand. To achieve this, a manager should help create clear social media policies and online responsibilities of the company and its target audience alike. Similarly, the community manager should make an active effort to respond to everyone. In so doing, the manger will identify the important members of the social media community. In other words, some social media users are more important to keep happy than others, particularly if they have thousands of followers who treat their opinions as facts.

By maintaining a helpful, authentic and always available online presence, the community manager will encourage polite engagement that raises a brand's visibility and profile. Recall the earlier discussions in this chapter regarding the fact that consumers trust brands that engage with them. Well, the online community manager is the job title that ensures that the engagement ends in a positive experience for both brands and consumers alike.

A great way to prepare yourself for this role is to simply be active online. Maybe try out being a community moderator of one of your favorite websites. If you enjoy the work, it is a good sign you would be a natural fit for this important job role.

## SOCIAL MEDIA ANALYST

**Required Skills**
- Tracking and Analyzing the Company's Online Media Presence
- Advise Brands on How to Better Improve Social Media Efforts Based on Proven Data
- Research Techniques and Tools Needed to Optimize Social Media Presence and Visibility
- Effective Communication Skills That Makes It Easy for C-Level Professionals to Understand How to Make Data-Driven Improvements
- Analyze Social Media for Competitor Threats and Activity

**Expected Salary: $50,000 to $65,000**

To effectively analyze social media for a company, a job candidate typically needs a background in analytics and/or data. Specifically, that background should have provided experience with interpreting key data and providing business analysis based on the data's interpretation. Social media hinges on this level of analysis. Companies are well aware of the fact that social media data, online data, and similar metrics have a significant influence on the company's financial performance. Just as importantly, these metrics have the ability to influence how people perceive the company's reputation.

A quality social media analyst can expect to interact with managers throughout the department since it is their analysis that will be used to determine the organization's strategies, goals, and long-term social media marketing visions. As such, this position requires an employee to be flexible and work well with plenty of departments involved with the company's social media efforts.

Perhaps most importantly of all, however, is the analyst's responsibility to constantly monitor, track and analyze the entirety of the brand's social media presence. Without quality data, a company cannot make the necessary improvements to better relate to a target audience. Once the data is gathered, however, the analyst must condense this information into easily digestible and actionable information. As such, the ability to make data and analytics quickly understandable to management is nearly as important as understanding analytics and gathering quality data. Effective communication skills are needed to help C-level professionals easily understand how to make data-driven improvements to company marketing efforts.

In addition to this critical responsibility, the analyst must also rev
iew and assess the social media presence of competitors. Learning from mistakes and/or successes of other competitors provides valuable information that can be passed to social media management.

The social media analyst, then, is best thought of as the trusted adviser management needs to make sure the department continues to excel.

## SOCIAL MEDIA MARKETING MANAGER

### Required Skills
- Guiding the Social Media marketing Department Toward Sustainable Success
- Overseeing the Company's Social Media Presence
- Analyze Data to Help Brands Make Actionable Decisions That Deliver Re-

sults
- Ensuring the Brand's Social Media Efforts Align with the Company's Overall Marketing KPI's
- An Established Track Record of Digital Marketing Success

**Expected Salary: $105,000 to $115,000**

Imagine that an entire social media department looks to you for guidance. That is the responsibility of the social media marketing manager. While the work of other employees in the department turn content ideas and campaign strategies into a reality, the final decision to move forward with any given marketing campaign or executing a particular strategies is the social media marketing manager's responsibility.

As a company's top social media specialist, this position needs a firm handle on every aspect of the company's social media efforts to make these critical decisions. To make these key decisions, the manager must be able to make sense of the data and analytics to make actionable improvements to future social media marketing campaigns. Other primary qualifications needed for this role include the abilities to manage the brand's overarching social media plan and overseeing the brand's social media presence on all channels and platforms.

A key qualification that stems from these responsibilities is the ability to work with the marketing department to create social media efforts that align with the brand's overall marketing/PR vision. Similarly, the marketing manager must also provide input to C-level executives on social media changes and emerging technology within the social media industry. As such, it is imperative that the manager maintains strong familiarity with all the latest trends in order to best track KPIs and similar data. Mastering these qualifications helps the manager and the brand stay a step ahead of the competition.

Given the job qualifications this role entails, any brand which places these responsibilities on an unproven digital marketer will likely come to regret the decision. This job title is for the battle-tested leaders of the social media space and digital marketing industry.

# DIRECTOR OF SOCIAL MEDIA

**Required Skills**

- Take the Responsibility of Heading the Entire Social Media Department
- Help All Social Media Teams Collaborate and Cross-Function as a Cohesive Whole
- Create Guidelines and Best Practices Used by the Entire Department
- Oversee All Daily Activities and Use Analytics to Analyze Results Both During and After Marketing Campaigns
- Create Weekly Reports that Provide Key Information for Other C-Level Executives Regarding the Social Media Team's Progress

**Expected Salary: $110,000 to $125,000**

The Director of Social Media runs the entirety of the social media department at a given organization. Years of experience give the director the knowledge needed to fulfill this job role, having already proved capable of helping companies experience social media growth.

The director helps all social media teams collaborate and cross-function to work as a cohesive whole, producing compelling content according to each brand's unique DNA and key performance indicators.

Along the way, the director creates the guidelines and best practices that guide the department. To make sure these goals are met, the director must also oversee daily activities and receive regular reports from the social media manager.

Both during and after marketing campaigns, the director takes a close look at what did and did not work as intended. Analytic expertise is essential to do so, but fortunately previous social media experience should guarantee the director already has these skills.

Finally, the director creates weekly social reports that inform other C-level executives on the social media team's progress and the results they are delivering for the company.

# VP OF MARKETING & SOCIAL MEDIA

### Required Skills

- Proven Leader in All Previous Social Media Roles
- Report Directly to the CEO and Formulate Strategies for Sustained Social Media Success
- Work Closely with the Director of Social Media to Make Sure the Right Strategies are Implemented
- Willing to Step in and Analyze the Data When Skilled Acumen is Needed
- An Established Track Record of Strategic Thinking and Long-Term Vision

### Expected Salary: $135,000+

This high-level position is typically the next promotion tier for successful directors of social media. It is customary for this role to report directly to the company CEO and/or other high-level execs. The VP works closely with the director and other managers to make sure the brand content and social media strategies are to his or her liking.

Realistically, the VP has the same skills as a director, only the VP has already proven him or herself in that role and all other jobs previously held.

While strategy is a key component of this role, the VP is more than capable of rolling up the sleeves and doing the hard work of data analysis on his or her own. In fact, it is not uncommon for them to do so when their uniquely skilled social media acumen is needed to make particularly important decisions.

Finally, the VP often works directly with any and all key clients and social media influencers, leveraging his or her high-level position to speak authoritatively to these key social media figures. While there is much appeal to this job title, the responsibilities are weighty. For candidates in the running for such a prestigious job title, however, it is likely they are more than comfortable with this level of responsibility.

# PERSONALIZING YOUR PATH TOWARD A SOCIAL MEDIA CAREER

While the previously mentioned job titles are far from the only job titles you will find within a social media department, they are among the most important ones. Finding your path in this field should be a personal journey that is uniquely yours. As an inspiration, take a look at how Bilal Jaffery used social media itself to take a job search risk and advance his career.

Enterasys was in need of a new Director of Social Marketing, so Enterasys hiring manager Vala Afshar appropriately sent out a blast on Twitter reading: "I am hiring a director of #marketing, focused on higher-ed; six figure salary, amazing team. Apply via Twitter. #jobs."

Why go looking for a skilled social media marketer on Twitter? As Afshar explained, mobile and social is all about a lifestyle, not just technology. Finding the best social media talent requires going where the conversation is to find the best talent who are already hyperconnected and social. Afshar intuitively knew he would find a top talent, and Bilal Jaffery proved him right.

Jaffery decided to participate in this unorthodox job search by applying for the position on Twitter with a #socialCV hashtag, clearly aware of the fact that a cover letter sent via social media is unusual. In his tweet, he highlighted an article on social strategy he wrote for Social MediaToday. One tweet later, the rest is history, and Bilal now leads Deloitte's digital strategy transformation effort.

Like Jaffery's fresh approach to landing a great social media marketing job, always focus on remaining consistent and unique while you network with the influencers who matter. In this way, you are setting yourself up for long-term and ongoing social media marketing success.

Take the information provided here and use it to inspire yourself. Find what speaks to you, and do not look back once you have found the path that takes you to the career you want. Every success story begins with a dream that is uniquely yours in the same way that Jaffery had a unique lens through which he viewed the Enterasys job search. Dream big and make this chapter the start of your own personalized social media marketing success story.

INTENTIONALLY LEFT BLANK

# 05

////////////////////////////////////////////////////////////

# FOR THE TECH-SAVVY DIGITAL MARKETER, A WEB ANALYTICS CAREER AWAITS

## WHAT YOU WILL LEARN IN THIS CHAPTER:

* What Makes Digital Analytics Essentially Recession-Proof
* What Questions a Digital Web Analyst Helps a Company Answer
* How Web Analytics Pros Make Sense of Petabytes Worth of Data
* How Digital Analytics Professionals Use Mathematics and Programming Skills to Collect and Extract Data
* Why Digital Analytics Job Seekers Should be Effective Interpreters
* The Two Likely Career Paths for a Digital Analytics Career
* How to Best Pursue a Career in Digital Analytics

In its most recent list of the "100 Best Jobs", US News and World Report included 6 analytics job titles in the list. The majority of those analytics positions included ties to digital marketing, highlighting the fact that digital analytics is a career of the future. The report ranked occupations based on job prospects, work-life balance, expected salary, and other important criteria.

For this reason, industry experts like Avinash Kaushik constantly field questions from readers asking how to break into the world of digital web analytics. Kaushik states that these interest levels are not surprising since the title of Web Analyst is essentially a recession-proof job. No political trend, new technology, or global economic occurrence has been able to slow the demand for web analysts, and it is unlikely that this demand will slow anytime soon. Perhaps, however, you are wondering why digital marketing efforts need to be measured in the first place. Digital marketing influencer Michael Brenner offers an excellent quote on why measuring results is so important. Brenner states that, in the world of digital marketing, "everything we do is digital. Everything digital is trackable. Because of this, there shouldn't be any waste within a marketing organization."

In other words, without measuring results, digital marketing organizations and entrepreneurs are wasting their time and effort. Digital marketing should be about providing proven results that businesses can value and see results from embracing. That only happens with measurement and data-driven analysis. Even Facebook likes or Instagram shares can be indicative of a marketing success, and by ignoring these numbers, brands lose out on valuable opportunities to assess growth areas and ways to improve.

Beyond the importance of measurement, broadly speaking, here are a few more reasons why digital web analysts are highly sought after commodities in the world of digital marketing.

First, they help digital marketing teams and businesses answer questions that are central to the entire digital marketing effort. Companies need to ask who visits their website and what those visitors do on the website when they do visit. A web analyst will provide the answers to these pressing questions. From there, the analysis builds toward answering other critical questions, including:

- What would the company like website visitors to do on their website? How should a visitor interact with the company?
- How can the company get visitors to do what the company needs them to do in order to profit?
- Once visitors start behaving the way a business needs, is there a way to make

them do it more frequently?

* How can visitors be encouraged to complete a sale for companies that sell products? Is a more attractive design or better written content needed?

Web analysts are the critical employees who provide answers to these seemingly simple questions. Without the expertise and experience of a savvy web analyst, a company's big data would largely go to waste. Just look at Walmart for an example, and you will see the value of a having a web analyst truly.

As the largest retailer in the world, Walmart has over 10,000 stores and almost half a trillion dollars in annual revenue to its name. With that size comes petabytes of data on an hourly basis. In fact, Walmart collects 2.5 petabytes of information from 1 million customers each and every hour. How large is a petabyte? One petabyte is the equivalent of 20 million filing cabinets of text, which is approximately 167 times the total number of books in the Library of Congress. Let that figure sink in for a moment. Every hour, Walmart collects data and information of this scope and volume.

With this information, Walmart is uniquely poised to capitalize on this information and turn it into actionable insights that help the brand grow. However, these benefits are only available if skilled web analysts and data analysts make sense of the data and turn it into comprehensive information executives can use. In Walmart's case, they are well aware of this need. That is why Neil Ashe, Walmart's CEO of Global eCommerce, says Walmart's mission statement is to "know what every product in the world is. We want to know who every person in the world is. And we want to have the ability to connect them together in a transaction."

Walmart tracks this information thanks to its technology research division known as Walmart Labs. The company uses their research division to turn vast amounts of sales data into information about individual customers. As such, data mining and using sophisticated technologies are at the heart of Walmart Labs' efforts. Most successful companies today are behaving similarly, even if they are not operating at the scope and scale of a Walmart.

# WHAT A WEB ANALYST IS EXPECTED TO DO, SPECIFICALLY

The general introduction into the questions a web analyst answers is a helpful and simplified introduction into what a web analyst does, but it is equally important to understand the specifics as to how a web analyst answers these questions. To simplify what is a complex discussion, it is helpful to discuss the scope of the web analyst role.

Simply put, web analytics is a multi-discipline endeavor that aims to quantify and measure marketing efforts on the web. More broadly, this means a web analyst is focused on analyzing and enhancing things like web usability, design, product sales, web content, and how website architecture is structured. In this way, a web analyst has his or her hands on just about every aspect of web analysis and marketing optimizations.

Achieving these lofty goals requires Google Analytics in conjunction with other tools like Omniture, IBM's Watson, CrazyEgg, or Hotjar. The web analyst is always looking for tools that will add value when used in combination with digital analytics, since these tools help businesses understand data and translate this enhanced understanding into meaningful marketing improvements. Why are these tools needed? Web analysis is mining an almost endless treasure trove of data, making analysis from one person, without the use of sophisticated technology to gather that data, impossible. Analytics tools are used to gather the data and organize the data in an intelligible way, and then the analyst uses his or her expertise working with these tools to turn the information into actionable plans for marketing improvements.

In this way, web analysts are an invaluably important element of a business's marketing efforts. The ability to turn complex data into actionable insights is what web analysis is all about, and it is the web analysts who deliver these insights to the C-Level execs, who then make decisions based on this valuable information.

## ANALYTICS FOR SMALL BUSINESS

Do not think of analytics as just for the large enterprise-level clients with seemingly endless revenue. Small businesses also need analytics to best their local competition and also compete with the larger businesses as well. In fact, it is small business that is often making the most innovative use of analytics in their marketing efforts. For one thing, small business is uniquely capable of showing the location-based benefits analytics and data can provide.

Dani Weiss is a Seattle wedding photographer who was getting precisely zero local interest about her business online. The problem was not a lack of demand for wedding photographers in the area. After all, people get married in a major metropolitan area like Seattle every day. Using analytics revealed that thousands of searches for Seattle wedding photographers occur every month.

The issue, then, was helping Dani's business stand out and get to the top of the Google results page. Dani reached out to a local business specializing in analytics to help her get there. This analytics-focused marketing business wanted two things for Dani's business. First, they wanted Dani Weiss Photography to show up on the first page of Google when people searched for "wedding photographer"-related keywords in Seattle in traditional search results. By traditional search results, I mean the results you will come across in any search. However, they also wanted her business to show up on the first page of Google maps results, a subsection of the first page of rankings that highlights local businesses.

These results were achieved for Dani through a comprehensive use of analytics. The company hired to help her researched popular search terms in the area and crosschecked those terms to see whether the terms could be found on Dani's website. Improvements were then made to both the website's text and user experience, based on what analytics revealed needed to be changed. Additional analysis was used to get Dani the needed links to respected websites that would make her professional site seem more authoritative. Finally, they added her business to trusted third-party directories commonly used by brides in the Seattle area and helped her implement a strategy to get more reviews to post on Google+.

The end result of this analytics-driven campaign was that Dani's website became the top local result in all of Seattle, helping her transform the small business from zero online leads to becoming the top result for a wide range of wedding photographer keywords. Just as important, she gained a 90% increase in web traffic and obtained 110% more leads via phone calls and emails. This is the power of using analytics to spot and assess areas of improvement for a small business's marketing efforts.

## SKILLS NEEDED FOR DIGITAL ANALYTICS

To start, a strong understanding of how the web works is of the utmost importance for someone looking to enter the field of digital analytics. From there, you will need to also understand the business itself, gaining familiarity with the customers it must attract and the business's target demographics. These types of analytical inquiries inform better interpretation of data and decision-making. In effect, digital analytics is much more about understanding and problem solving than it is merely math-driven. As such, do not be scared away from this field if math is not your favorite subject.

## STILL, TAKING SOME DATA-DRIVEN MATH COURSES WILL HELP YOU SUCCEED

Of course, it would not hurt to take a few data-driven math courses that will give you experience with analyzing and interpreting data if you are still in school. Data analysts are expected to have quantitative insights into survey data, financial data, website metrics, ad-performance data, and more. All these data sets must be incorporated into accurate reports that are concise and easy for managers to digest. Even so, it is possible to be a great digital analytics professional merely by understanding technical tools and how the web works.

## HONE AND REFINE YOUR TECHNICAL EXPERTISE

Since technical knowledge of analytics tools and how to apply them in this field is also a must, begin shoring up your technical knowledge now. Pick a few analytics tools and start experimenting now on your own. Popular tools like Google Analytics and Piwik are free tools that will give you great experience and a head start learning some of the technical skills a web analyst will need. Even better, there are plenty of books, training, and free educational resources that will help you take a do-it-yourself approach to learning the technical side of this job role. These books and resources are discussed in a later section of this book, so if you are convinced by the end of this chapter that this field is for you, skip ahead and check out those resources. Not only is teaching yourself in tandem with learning from the experts a proven way to learn these skills, it is also a far more rewarding learning strategy. Instead of leaving your knowledge to lectures and books, working with these tools will give you hands-on trial and error experience as you go. In the long run, this will make you a better web analyst.

## PROBLEM SOLVERS ARE HIGHLY DESIRED IN DIGITAL ANALYTICS

Additionally, it is helpful if digital analysts have effective problem solving skills. One of the best ways to stand out as an analyst is to have a curious nature and recognize problem areas of the business before diving into the treasure troves of data. Recognizing some of these problems before analyzing the data provides a roadmap to assess and spot particular business vulnerabilities that can be turned into opportunities and quality returns on investment for the company. In this way, these beneficial problem solving skills are like having a treasure map before you go searching. It is always best to know what you are looking for before starting the search, and digital analysts with these skills are sure to be desirable employees that quickly rise up the ranks.

## COMMUNICATE CLEARLY AND CONCISELY TO IMPRESS C-LEVEL EXECUTIVES

Finally, a digital analyst needs to be more than just a problem solver and data expert. Communicating what you know in a clear and concise way is just as important. As mentioned, this job role will have you creating reports that condense vast amounts of information into easy to read and assess charts and performance benchmarks. Do not expect management and company executives to always greet an analyst's reports with open arms and enthusiasm. If a report is overly pessimistic and skeptical, executives may be reticent to embrace the report even if it is 100% accurate. For this reason, the best web analysts do more than just gather the data and report on it. They also know how to present an argument and defend it, even in the company board room.

Not only should a web analyst create reports backed by their interpretation of the data, they should also be ready to advise executives on what the next step should be. Whether the company needs further investment in a given resource, less investment, or a new strategy and change of company direction, web analysts are the ones who must make that case.

Be a storyteller when it is time to present your findings. Whether you choose to tell your story with a presentation, infographics, or data visualizations, make sure the insights will resonate in a compelling way. A data analyst should always focus on presenting data that connects to the goals of the business. Job candidates who can take complex math and distil it down into understandable talking points will be loved by managers and companies around the world. Such skillsets are exceedingly rare, and if you possess these skills, know that you will thrive as a web analyst or any other digital analytics professional.

## CHOOSING THE PATH FOR YOUR DIGITAL ANALYTICS CAREER

If web analytics is calling your name, know that there are two separate and distinct career paths you may wish to pursue. In many cases, a career in digital analytics will eventually take you to a crossroads where you must choose between continuing down the technical path of analytics or transitioning into the business side of the field. Those who remain on the technical side of digital analytics will eventually blossom into team leaders and managers, whereas moving into the business side of the company will lead to marketing managerial roles that still rely on digital analytics expertise.

As you can imagine, choosing this path is not a decision you will need to make now. Regardless, it is something to keep in mind as you learn and grow in this field, and it is far from an easy choice. If you are faced with this decision down the road, take the time to evaluate your strengths and the areas in which you excel. For example, if you are less comfortable with the communication skills needed in analytics, a transition into marketing may not be ideal. Sticking on the technical side will ensure you are overseeing employees who are comfortable speaking the language of complex mathematics and data analysis. Conversely, if you are a masterful communicator, a transition to the marketing and business side could be the best career choice you could make. No matter which path you choose, here are a few likely job titles to aspire to that may provide a rewarding and fruitful career.

## WEB ANALYST

### Required Skills
- Conduct Market Analysis of Industry Trends and Statistical Data
- Experience Working With Prominent Analytics Tools
- Capable of Researching Independently
- Design and Build Statistical Reports Based on the Data
- Clear Communication of the Relevance of All Data Analysis
- Effective Communication Skills are Needed to Present Data Analysis Findings

### Expected Salary: $45,000 to $60,000

The web analytics analyst is the entry-level position into the world of analytics. This position requires an ability to conduct market analysis on industry trends and statistical data important to the company's digital marketing efforts. Conducting this analysis requires using prominent analytics tools such as Adobe Analytics and Google Analytics, just to name a couple of the essential tools. Using these tools, the analyst is expected to be capable of independent research that expands the company's web analytics insights.

No matter what tools an employer expects the analyst to use, the analyst must then also be capable of designing, building, and delivering statistical reports based on what the data says. Analysts must then communicate the findings of these reports in clear and concise ways to business management and/or stakeholders.

Effectively, the analyst's primary role is to compile relevant data, and then explain how the data is relevant to the brand's marketing efforts. While an entry-level position, this key responsibility makes web analysts some of the most important professionals in all of digital marketing.

# WEB ANALYTICS SPECIALIST

**Required Skills**
- Provide Brands with the Right Information at the Right Time
- Stay Up to Date on the Latest Analytics Trends
- Create Detailed Reports that Help Brands Make Sense of Forecasts, Goal Progression and KPIs
- Report Directly to the Web Analytics Manager
- Help Clients Plan and Strategize Based on Data

**Expected Salary: $60,000 to $80,000**

When brands have the right information at the right time, great marketing strategies become a reality. The web analytics specialist is a key player in making sure brands have this level of analytics insight through the use of data.

The web analytics specialist prioritizes staying up to date on the latest analytics trends, using their working knowledge of Google Analytics and other tools to show stakeholders why following the data is a must. Further, the analytics specialist should be capable of setting up customized dashboards and assisting with creating and executing digital analytics strategies.

What kind of strategies? For starters, the analyst should be able to conceptualize and develop targets and goals for things like engagement funnels.

Effectively, the specialist creates detailed reports that help the business have more detailed forecasts, better information on goal progression and enhanced understandings of key performance indicators. As such, the specialist is expected to work closely with developers on important products and touch points for the brand.

This job is typically the next step up from the entry-level analyst role, which entails the responsibility of reporting directly to the web analytics manager. Given this added responsibility, it is not uncommon for the web analytics specialist to be tasked with presenting data-driven analysis to clients, as well as assisting clients with planning and strategic directions to take based on data.

# WEB ANALYTICS MANAGER

## Required Skills

- Analyze Website and Digital Channel Performance (Social, Paid Search, Display Advertising, and SEO)
- Supporting Cross Channel Strategies to Maximize Customer Satisfaction
- Understanding the Customer Journey and How They are Expected to Interact with the Company/Brand/Website at Different Stages
- Make Sense of Data Quickly, Helping Brands Leverage Data into Actionable Opportunities
- Effective Communication Skills are Needed to Present Data Analysis Findings

## Expected Salary: $90,000 to $115,000

The digital analytics manager is the critical management member who actively oversees the data and data analysis processes. In large companies, a manager is responsible for number crunching, checking up on the work of junior analysts, and ensuring that reports are accurate and properly prepared. In small companies with a one-team analyst department, the digital analyst professionals carry this load all by themselves.

Either way, this position needs to coordinate with other departments that provide some of the data a digital analyst needs to actually perform their job function. When other departments are lagging on this front, it is the manager's job to make sure that this data is obtained as soon as possible so the company does not lose out on valuable time to gain actionable insights.

Managers may also need to explore new areas of data to find areas of data worth investigating, to determine if new and helpful trends can be discovered. For example, Macy's used data analytics to adjust pricing in nearly real time for a staggering 73 million items. This technology was provided by SAS Institute, and the price shifts were based on demand and company inventory. However, it is likely that the company did not seek out SAS Institute for the outsourced technology until a digital analytics manager spotted the potential benefits of this pricing technology within the company's existing data.

How can a manager help companies better understand this data? There are a few ways this goal is realized. First, the manager must develop a strong business acumen over the course of his or her career. Turning numbers into actionable insights must happen fast in a rapidly moving business competing with other brands in the industry, so time is money when it comes to making sense of the data. While the manager pushes analysts to work quickly, it is just as important for the manager to push analysts to get the right answers.

According to industry expert Avinash Kaushik, the core problem of most data analytics tools today is that they gather a ton of data that tells you very little without the expertise of a proven data analytics professional. The manager will challenge the findings of their team of analysts and will constantly question the conclusions derived from the data. In this way, when data findings are presented to professionals in the conference room, the data has been properly vetted and fact-checked to increase the odds that the analysis is accurate.

## DIGITAL ANALYTICS DIRECTOR

**Required Skills**
- Lead the Analytics Team and Motivate the Team to Put in Their Best Work
- Strong Analytics Experience is a Must
- Work With Other Department Heads and Agencies to Make High-Level Recommendations for the Business
- Always Looking to Extract Data and Utilize It in Innovative Ways Using the Latest Technology
- Making Meaningful Improvements Based on Key Performance Indicators (KPIs)

**Expected Salary: $120,000 to $140,000**

This position has the task of leading the analytics team. This role requires strong analytics experience, and as a team director, this person must also motivate others to do their best work. Beyond being a motivational leader with a strong grasp of analytics, this position also requires the director to have a deep understanding of the business. How the business is structured and organized will reveal its fundamental requirements and needs. In turn, this information is used to develop more sophisticated analytics tools that better address the needs of the business.

For example, understanding who the business needs to target to drive up revenue will affect how a digital analytics director runs a given campaign or analysis of the data. For example, financial institution American Express recognized that hindsight-oriented analytics was not helping their business. They needed to get out in front and discover indicators that could predict customer loyalty, so they got to work developing predictive models that analyzed historical transactions and other variables. Now, the company believes it can identify nearly 1 in 4 Australian financial accounts that will close within the next four months. These insights likely occurred because a digital analytics director was able to pinpoint the unique needs and requirements of the business, and then data analytics was used to address those issues.

Part of understanding the requirements of the business involves working with other department heads and agency leaders within the company. This way, all departments operate as a team and part of a cohesive whole that is operating in the best interests of the business. The director is also tasked with making high-level recommendations and presentations to C-suite executives to provide the big picture of how digital analytics is helping the company achieve its goals.

Finally, a digital analytics director is tasked with taking a look at the key performance indicators (KPIs). A KPI, for reference, is a tracking measurement that affects a company's marketing objectives. Common KPIs that an analytics director pays close attention to include ROI (return on investment), website conversion rate, cost per lead by source, revenue per lead by source, and the % of sales derived from digital. Taken as a whole, these performance indicators present a clear snapshot of where the company is currently, and where they need to improve in order to meet marketing goals.

## DIGITAL CHIEF INFORMATION OFFICER ✪✪✪✪✪

### Required Skills
* A Proven Career Track Record of Making Sense of Complex Data, Providing Value to Both Employers and Clients
* Create the Strategies and Overall Vision for the Company's Analytics and Technology
* Ensure the Company has the Resources to Meet its Digital Marketing and IT

Goals
- Have the Acumen Needed to Position Your Company as a Digital Transformation Leader
- The Ability and Desire to Keep Your Company on the Cutting-Edge as Digital Marketing and IT Continue to Evolve

**Expected Salary: $150,000+**

The best data analysts in an organization have made a career out of making sense of complex data. Their strategies and concise interpretations have added immense value for their employer and their clients with a longstanding track record of success.

The very best data analysts who work their way up to director can ultimately aspire to becoming the Chief Information Officer, a job title that carries plenty of prestige and responsibility. The CIO is ultimately responsible for creating the ideas, strategies and vision for a company's analytics and technology.

This weighty responsibility involves working to ensure the company has the technological resources needed for effective digital marketing, aligning the business's IT infrastructure with the company's overall goals.

The CIO is increasingly a digital service-based role as much as it is an IT responsibility, which is why digital analytics professionals are increasingly in demand for this prestigious position. If you aspire to reach the rank of CIO, know that you will be given the responsibility of positioning your company as a leader in digital transformation. Given the rapid changes happening in digital marketing and the digital sector overall, this is an exciting role to take on that will keep you on the cutting-edge of industry change.

## TAKE CHARGE OF YOUR LIFE AND PURSUE DIGITAL ANALYTICS IF IT'S CALLING YOUR NAME

To conclude this chapter, I want to reiterate to you that now is the best time to jump into this field. If analytics is calling your name and the blend of math, programming, and communication skills required excite you, do not shy away from the challenge. While some people may hear "numbers" and pass on this career, you are not one of those people. The challenge should inspire you to reach out and take the career you want. Jobs are waiting for you in this field, and you simply need to put in the hard work to get those jobs. Take a look at how Annie Cushing has succeeded in this field for tangible evidence of how hard work pays off.

Annie is one of the world's foremost and independent Google Analytics experts. More importantly, at her website annielytics.com, she has a way of making analytics simple, fun, and accessible to newcomers. Perhaps that is because Annie herself was a newcomer to the industry not too long ago, and she wants to pass that knowledge on to readers who are as excited to start in this field. Annie's goal, as stated on her website, is to make data sexy and fun, which it is. Data are one of the best ways to see how your hard work and efforts in digital marketing lead others to take your advice and improve their brands as a result. I highly recommend browsing Annie's website and checking out her concise and highly readable blog posts. You will learn a great deal and have fun while doing it.

What is stopping you from achieving your dream position in digital marketing and web analytics? Nothing. If it is a position in digital analytics that you want, go out and get it. Once you finish this book (or even this chapter!) and determine digital analytics is the field for you, go out and start doing. The old adage that one learns by doing is especially important for the hopeful web analyst. Start a blog that highlights your journey into the new and exciting world of analytics, and maybe even follow the roadmap paved by bloggers and industry experts like Annie Cushing and Romy Misra. Romy got started by taking publicly available data and used public analysis via popular analytics tools. Then, Romy published the results on her blog. Not only was this a brave foray into the world of analytics, it also served as a compelling resume for any potential employer who wanted to see the skills Romy had. You may wish to do the same. If so, write about your successes, your trials and your errors. Not only will you be learning by doing, but you will also broadcast to the world what you have learned in this field, while doing something you love that inspires you.

Additionally, do not discount the value of classroom courses as you continue to learn by doing. Focused MS programs in business analytics from a quality university (like this business analytics program from NYU) will give you a focused, honed curriculum designed to give you cutting-edge skills and re-al-world applications that will help you hit the ground running after earning your degree.

INTENTIONALLY LEFT BLANK

////////////////////////////////////////////////////////////

# SEARCHING FOR A DIGITAL MARKETING CAREER? CONSIDER SEARCH MARKETING

## WHAT YOU WILL LEARN IN THIS CHAPTER:

* How Search Marketing and Display Advertising Complement One Another
* Why Search Marketing is a Priority for Almost Any Business (Which Means Jobs for You)
* Why Search Marketers and Display Advertisers Must Think About the Target Audience at All Times
* The Unifying Theme That Binds Search Marketing and Display Advertising
* What Career Paths Are Available When Pursuing Search Marketing and/or Display Advertising
* How Search Marketing in Theory Differs From Search Marketing in Reality (and Why the Distinction Matters for Your Career)

Decades ago, large sprawling billboards on highways were (and still are, for the largest of brands) a great way to get attention for a brand's products.

With the internet, even the smallest brands can implement effective SEM and display advertising campaigns to reap similar results, all on a modest budget with effective digital marketing strategy. Because of the ways in which the world has changed, search ads and display advertising now make up nearly half of the digital ad spending in the United States. To be exact, the figure is 47.9%, which equates to $32.17 billion.

Search engine marketing, like all things digital marketing, is a relatively new career option. Having been around for only the past 15 years or so, it is already an important career path in the world of digital marketing. In fact, search engine marketing is now so important that nearly every business is familiar with the importance of paid ads and media buys. To take just one example, retail advertisers spent a staggering $1.44 billion on Google text ads in the fourth-quarter of 2015 during the holiday season.

Why has SEM and display advertising become a priority for almost every business with an online presence? Simply put, businesses need visibility online in order to reach their customers, and search engine marketing gives businesses the visibility they need to thrive. Using paid placement to showcase quality ads on Google search results provides businesses with enhanced visibility and, when done correctly, improved sales metrics.

Wrapping your head around the big picture of search and display advertising requires an understanding of paid ad placement and why businesses rely on this digital marketing strategy. To gain a basic framework of understanding SEM, Google Adwords is as good a place to start as any. By most measures, Google Adwords is the most popular platform utilized by search marketers. The way SEM works on a platform like Google Adwords is that advertisers make bids on keywords that Google users might use when looking for certain products and services online. By bidding on these keywords, advertisers will enjoy the opportunity of having their ads appear alongside those search results.

A common term for ads of this nature are called pay-per-click (PPC) advertisements. There is no one-size approach to PPC ads. Some may be text-based, others may be designed to showcase a product in a visually striking way using a combination of text and visual imagery. Google has a wide range of ad types that are offered via Google Adwords, which you have no doubt seen if you use Google for your search engine. From Google shopping ads to call-only ads that provide business names with a phone number to call, there are plenty of ways to get a brand's message out there with PPC. Now that you have a framework of what paid ads and SEM entails, the bigger question is why brands care to market in this manner.

Well, for starters, you are reaching motivated customers. Imagine a tech aficionado enters a google search for "best 4k TVs." If research reveals this is a popular search term for motivated TV buyers, an electronics store would be wise to bid on this keyword. By doing so, the brand would be reaching motivated TV buyers who are ready to purchase a product. Then, with an eye-catching and textually relevant ad, motivated traffic can be driven to the brand's website to complete the sale.

Another integrally important area of focus in this chapter is the digital marketing strategy of display advertising. So, just what is display advertising exactly? Display ads are often large advertisements found on websites, but the ads are always designed to make a bold and eye-catching statement about the brand to a website visitor. Essentially, these ads appear on distinct parts of a website that are reserved for advertising, and they typically are designed with branding in mind. However, they are also used for improving a brand's conversion rate. This form of advertising may rely on traditional banner ads, retargeting ads, large text billboards, or video content. Of each of these types of content, you may be least familiar with retargeting ads. Think of retargeting ads as "ads that follow you" in much the same way that annoying ex-partner you cannot seem to get out of your life. The key difference is that these ads are meant to be unobtrusive. Rather, they subtly keep track of website visitors and, when those visitors go to another website, they will be shown a retargeting ad that is designed to bring you back to their website to complete a purchase.

While the format and implementation of display advertising varies, the general idea is that this form of content advertising is an outstanding complement to native advertising. For a time, some display advertising skeptics believed the days of display advertising would soon come to an end. The reason for their skepticism, which has now been shown to be misguided, was based on the rise of native advertising. Native advertising, in contrast to display advertising, is a form of disguised advertising that is meant to blend in with its surroundings. Take Facebook Ads as an example of the difference between display advertising and native advertising. In Facebook's feed, the advertisement will appear as just any regular Facebook post, but it is actually sponsored. These ads work well because they appear naturally on the page and are non-invasive, which led some to conclude that banner ads and the like were on the way out. Innovations in digital advertising have proven these doubters wrong.

Today, banner advertisements and similar display advertising formats are used to tell the story of content in uniquely exciting ways. Natural storytellers will find much to love about a career in display advertising as a result. Display advertising used effectively should tap into what is known as sequential advertising, which is the idea of using one ad to inform the next one. For example, think about how Gifs (animated images) are used online. Brands can use animated images to tell stories that a single image simply cannot. Wise display advertising uses these capabilities to maximum advantage by showcasing humor, personality, or even multiple angles of the same product to create stunning product showcases. When done effectively, display advertising can, similar to SEM, deliver rapid marketing results.

While SEM and display advertising are exceptionally similar, there are slight but important distinctions between the two forms of digital marketing. The simplest explanation is that SEM is about pay-per-click ads, and display advertising is about banner ads. As such, SEM is used for advertising through search engines, whereas banner ads can be used on websites and on Facebook where image ads are used. Both, used in tandem, can be powerful as we will see in the next case study.

As opposed to SEO (which will be discussed in later chapters) and other forms of digital marketing that take time to produce tangible benefits, the ROI on effective SEM and display marketing is far more immediate. Brands that tap into "on the rise" keywords are capable of dramatically transforming their business by getting in on landscape shifts in respective industries and industry sectors. A classic example of this can be shown by a case study involving Airbnb, a brand that went from an industry upstart to one of the world's leading accommodation providers via home sharing.
Landscape shifts like these are an ongoing aspect of life in the digital world. As with all things digital, search marketing is in a constant state of flux.

When businesses identify these shifts and adapt to them, it can make a world of difference. Airbnb did not start out as the global brand it is now known as today. In its early years, Airbnb had difficulty breaking through in the search rankings in countries like Germany, where other German rental websites had a few years of a head start. The age of a website is one of several factors that affect search rankings, and Airbnb was at a decided disadvantage here. Airbnb charted a creative path to rise up the rankings.

To do so, they outspent competitors via Google AdWords in an attempt to outdo competitors for generic keyword rankings such as "German vacation rentals" and "Berlin vacation homes." Second, the brand recognized the importance of display advertising (more on this career path in just a second). Airbnb understood that a quality click-through rate requires more than just a high search ranking. Even if a brand gets on the first page of a Google, a desktop or mobile user may still choose to click on a different link if it is written in a more effective way. Quality display advertising ensures that a brand's given search result is both well written and visually appealing, thereby increasing the chances a user will click through to the brand's website. Airbnb recognized this need and invested in Google display advertising with banner campaigns that included attractive images from actual housing offers on their website. As a result, the display advertising ultimately increased the effectiveness of the content users saw when they found Airbnb, which led to better ROI. By incorporating these strategies, Airbnb enjoyed remarkable success considering their online competitors had been around far longer.

## WHAT JOB SKILLS DOES SEARCH MARKETING REQUIRE?

Search engine marketing requires a unique skillset and a unique personality to match. Why might you consider this promising career path as your first foray into the world of digital marketing? For one thing, the barriers to entry are reasonable, making it a great choice for those in career transition as well as recent graduates alike. Search engine marketing is primarily concerned with improving marketing results based on Google Adwords, and the good news is there is a wealth of training resources available for free or at little cost. There are plenty of ways to get the training you need, so do not let the fear of learning something new put you off from a career that offers stability, good pay, and job security.

Since SEM is such a necessary component for most businesses, this career path is a great launching pad into other marketing careers over time. So long as businesses need to get people to buy products, services or interact with their brand online, the skills you learn as a search marketer will be valued.

While Adwords expertise is a core aspect of SEM, it is very important to also master the ability to copywrite and make landing pages. Using Unbounce drag and drop tools to move any element of a landing page or overlay will help an SEM professional quickly improve the look and feel of a page without needing to use code. Everything from the Call to Action to a key image on the page can be moved around with ease, and the SEM professional ought to be familiar with maximizing the benefits provided by these tools.

SEM also requires marketers to familiarize themselves with data metrics so their decisions are always backed by the data. This helps in boardroom presentations and the like, so a career in this field is served well by any digital marketing role that familiarizes you with data tracking and analysis. Advancing through the ranks of an SEM department requires being able to assess clickthrough reports, purchases, and similarly desirable outcomes on a regular basis.

If you are enticed by the easy access to training that makes it relatively easy to enter this field, know that the one job skill that is non-negotiable for a prospective search marketing professional is passion for the field. A genuine commitment to this field will give you the enthusiasm needed to learn valuable skills like a/b testing, conversion tracking, and custom reporting, all of which will help you stand out and advance your career. Fortunately, it is easy to get the certifications you need to gain basic skills that will help you land a job in this field before advancing to higher end skillsets. Google offers Adwords certification, which is an extremely valuable tool for students who want to pursue a career in this field. Additionally, it looks great on a resume! No matter where your career in digital marketing takes you, so long as you remain passionate about getting to know your audience, your brand, and the goals you want to achieve, the sky is the limit.

## SKILLS WILL YOU NEED IN DISPLAY ADVERTISING

For display advertising, do not think that merely having well-designed banner ads and visuals are all that this career involves. It is certainly true that a big function of display advertising careers is creating valuable banners that make a campaign and brand stand out in a positive way. A good design is just one element of successful display advertising. Think of display advertising as a movie with beautiful Hollywood stars. While the good looks of the stars in the film will help sell the movie in theaters, a good script, quality directing, and skillful cinematography are also of great importance. Simply put, there is more to display advertising than good looks.

## ALWAYS KEEP THE TARGET AUDIENCE IN MIND

For starters, a display advertiser needs to keep the target audience in mind at all times. Targeting an audience who has already demonstrated interest in a brand's products or services will go a long way toward increasing conversion rates via display advertising. To that end, display advertisers need to be skilled at targeting. For example, a great banner ad for Diet Coke is going to resonate with an audience focused on cutting calories. With online tools, advertisers can find people who are actively reading weight loss blogs and target individuals looking to cut back on their caloric intake. Combining great visuals with the right audience, then, is a great way to increase the likelihood of success.

## AN ANALYTICAL MIND IS A GREAT WAY TO SEPARATE YOURSELF FROM PEERS

Additionally, having an analytical mind is a good skill to have as a marketer. Why? Marketers need to read reports and make key decisions based on their analysis. Over the course of your career in this field, you will need to learn how to exclude ad placements that are a waste of your company ad budget, while keeping a watchful eye on ad placement reports and SEM. These reports will give you the insight needed to track user behavior and see where a brand's recipe for success lies in the world of display advertising. Practically, this means a marketer will have the insight needed to know whether it is best to bid high, stop a bid, or even kill an ad campaign. Reading SEM reports is just as useful for measuring conversion rates and ROI.

## MASTER THE NUANCES OF MOBILE VS. DESKTOP

Display advertisers should also pay attention to tracking metrics and data over both mobile devices and desktop computers. Ads that work well on mobile may not perform as well on desktop, and the opposite is also true. Ads that work well on desktop may not work well on mobile.

## KNOW WHAT RETARGETING IS AND HOW TO WIELD IT EFFECTIVELY

Another core component worth mentioning in detail is a display advertiser's retargeting responsibilities. Retargeting is a fancy term used to describe bringing website visitors who did not make a purchase back to the website. For example, say you are browsing a clothing retailer's website for a new shirt. You look at a few shirts and other clothing items, and you were interested in the shirts, but you ultimately leave the website without making a purchase. A week later, you are browsing another clothing website for shirts, but you receive an advertisement that displays relevant shirts you had looked at previously on the original website. This, in essence, is retargeting at work, and a display advertising manager's job is to create compelling ads that retarget previous website visitors and compel them to return to the website and buy the brand's products. Only a small percent of web traffic converts on a first-time visit, so retargeting is arguably one of a display advertiser's most important responsibilities. Often, display ad expertise is paired with SEM department expertise since improved search engine results are an important element of getting display advertising noticed more effectively.

## SEM MASTERY OCCURS WHEN FORM MATCHES FUNCTION

In short, display advertisers need to match form with function. Making great banners and visuals is one thing (form), but targeting users and providing them with relevant results is another matter (function). Display advertisers that combine form and function are going to be highly sought after commodities over the course of their career. If you loved seeing Don Draper do his thing on Mad Men, you are probably a good fit for a career in display advertising. Like Don Draper, display advertisers have a natural eye for what appeals to users, an intellectual curiosity for where the world is headed (data trends) and a love for telling a good story. If this sounds like you, display advertising may be the ideal way to get your start in digital marketing.

## THE FOUNDATIONAL CORE THAT UNIFIES CAREERS IN SEARCH MARKETING AND DISPLAY ADVERTISING

While there are certainly tangible differences between search marketing and display advertising careers, both require a strong core appreciation for the whole of internet marketing. As mentioned, a search engine marketer must think about things like effective content that delivers marketing results, proven research strategies, and similar best practices to do their job effectively. In this way, search engine marketing bleeds into other areas of digital marketing, as is so often the case in this rapidly evolving industry.

Display advertising is no different. We have already discussed how an eye for data trends and telling a good story are critical aspects of display advertising. The lesson here is that, while digital marketing jobs are categorized and divided into different sectors, there is still a great degree of overlap for almost any digital marketing position. Both these areas of digital marketing are closely related enough that a nuanced understanding of both fields is going to be necessary for anyone who wants a lasting career in either display advertising or SEM. The reason for this is many ad campaigns integrated both of these strategies in a coordinated effort, like the Airbnb study referenced.

This is a classic example of businesses not putting all their eggs in one basket when it comes to marketing strategy. Search engine marketers and display advertising pros alike both need to be aware of the business's overarching advertising and marketing goals/strategies. As such, overlap and flexibility is a hallmark of this industry that keeps things fresh and exciting.

Master this foundational core, and you are on your way to SEM success. Below are some of the job titles in the SEM that you can aspire to reach as your career progresses.

# SEARCH MARKETING/DISPLAY ADVERTISING COORDINATOR

### Required Skills

- Support the SEM/Display Ad Team
- Learn All Pertinent Elements of the Company's SEM and Display Advertising Strategy
- Learn Future Skills that will be Applicable for Future Promotions
- Create Monthly Client Visibility Reports and Linking Programs
- Diligently Perform Tasks Passed Down by Senior Members in the Department

### Expected Salary: $35,000 to $50,000

Search engine marketing and display advertising coordinators play an important supporting role to their respective teams. As entry-level positions, these jobs are a great way to begin mastering the skills needed to advance a career and climb the ladder.

Both coordinator titles will require supporting the more senior analysts/specialists within the department with strategic planning for clients. The goal at this stage is for the coordinator to learn all pertinent elements of SEM and display advertising. In this way, think of the coordinator role as a crucial support piece who is learning future skills that will be utilized if they perform well enough to earn a promotion.

Creating monthly client visibility reports, creating linking programs, and assisting with one-off tasks that are passed down by senior team members are all part and parcel of the job description. As such, coordinators would be wise to treat this position as a time to update SEM and display advertising knowledge in order to keep current on the latest trends that may apply in their employer's field.

# SEARCH MARKETING SPECIALIST/DISPLAY ADVERTISING SPECIALIST

### Required Skills

* Manage the Daily Operation of a Search Campaign or Display Advertising
* For SEM Specialists, Grow Traffic, Revenue and Subscribers for the Brand
* For Display Specialists, Work with Large Data Sets to Create Sophisticated Advertising Solutions
* The Ability to be Both Creative and Data-Driven
* The Desire to Search for Answers and Problem Solve When Solutions Are Not Readily Apparent

### Expected Salary: $50,000 to $70,000

The search engine marketing specialist is tasked with managing the daily operations of a search campaign. The goals of a specialist are to grow traffic, revenue and subscribers for the brand.

A display advertising specialist, alternatively, ought to be adept at working with large data sets to create sophisticated advertising solutions that set the brand up for sustained success. This requires working with advanced technologies capable of advanced behavioral targeting, ad re-targeting, and real-time bidding.

Both professionals serve critical roles in a digital marketing department, reporting directly to their respective managers. Serving as a specialist in these fields require professionals to be both data-driven and creative. The common ground both of these titles share is the ability to look for answers and problem solve when solutions are far from obvious.

SEM and display advertising specialists who master their craft are the marketing manager's best friends. Establish yourself as a proven specialist, and it may not be long until you earn a promotion to manager.

# SEM/DISPLAY ADVERTISING MARKETING MANAGER

**Required Skills**

- Overseeing the SEM/Display Advertising Department Performance, which Includes Developing and Optimizing Ad Campaigns
- Achieve the Best Possible ROI Based on Budget
- Negotiating with Various Sources for the Best Deals on Purchases
- Staying on Top of Ad Buy Results in Order to Improve Results
- Effectively Lead and Inspire the Rest of the Department to Put in Their Best Work

**Expected Salary: $80,000 to $90,000**

According to ZenithOptimedia, the demand for SEM and display advertising specialists and professionals is high, thanks to the fact that display advertising has recently been proven to be the fastest growing sub-category of internet spending. This assertion is confirmed by global advertising trends, which are backed up by the 2014 report from ZenithOptimedia. This research forecast that displays advertising has a 15% annual growth forecast through 2018. This translates to jobs, and few jobs are in higher demand than SEM/display advertising managers.

Couple the fact that the internet is the fastest growing advertising medium with the rise of SEM and display advertising, and it is easy to see why large digital marketing departments make it a priority to hire SEM and display executives. Both SEM and display advertising managers are tasked with developing and optimizing their respective campaigns, which requires achieving the best possible ROI for the company.

Display advertising professionals need to have negotiation skills in order to negotiate ad space purchases. It does not help a business much if they are constantly getting fleeced on every purchase they make. It is a display advertising manager's responsibility to make sure the company gets a fair deal in these negotiations. Similarly, an SEM manager must also contemplate the ideal path forward when it comes to executing an effective search engine strategy. A strong understanding of bidding techniques and statistical analysis is needed for the SEM manager to make these big decisions.

In addition to negotiating, a manager must also oversee the results of their ad buys in order to optimize current and future campaigns. Additional job duties include require overseeing the totality of the display ad/SEM campaign programs and performance as well as optimizing user experiences throughout the campaign for improved conversion rates. Making these goals a reality demands the ability to effectively manage, lead, and inspire the display ad and SEM department teams to create quality ad placements and do their best work.

## DIRECTOR OF PAID SEARCH/ADVERTISING

### Required Skills

- Lead the SEM/Display Ad Team
- Creative Thinking and an Ability to Make the Brand's Big Decisions
- Familiarity with Data-Driven Analysis on a Regular Basis
- Thinking About Cost-Effective Strategies and ROI, Not Just Results
- The Capacity to Thrive in a High-Pressure Job Environment

### Expected Salary: $100,000 to $125,000

It is not an exaggeration to say that search engine marketers and display advertisers are some of the most necessary marketing specialists in the entirety of digital marketing. According to Digital Marketing Institute, SEM specialists are among the most sought after specialists in digital marketing, so it stands to reason that SEM professionals are also highly pursued at the executive level.

Creative thinking and outside the box solutions are a must for these professionals, and these skills led them to promotions each step of the way toward this title. An SEM director or display ad director uses the department's allotted budget to help the brand stand out with quality paid ad placements on Google and other prominent search engines like Bing and Yahoo. To do this requires working with SEM specialists and display advertisers throughout the department to ensure that keywords are tested, analyzed, and tracked to ensure site visits, purchases, and similar behaviors give the brand needed results.

Choosing the right search terms is not just about getting results. Executives must also think about what is cost-effective when it comes to the budget. The most effective paid search term may also double as the most expensive. From an ROI perspective, it may make more sense to investigate the possibility of bidding on less expensive and more efficient terms that will drive similar sales and conversion figures, albeit with a greater ROI.

Finally, an SEM manager must be able to see the big picture in a way that allows them to make the hard decisions. Imagine you are the manager and are faced with a dwindling ad budget and the reality that the ads you have already placed are not generating results. Do you decide to simply pull the ads and use what is left of the budget on new ads based on the data analysis? Alternatively, do you opt to stay a bit more patient if you believe there is solid data indicating that the ads will produce given a bit more time? These are the types of decisions facing an SEM manager, so the ability to thrive in a high-pressure environment while making the tough calls is critical.

## VP OF GROWTH & PERFORMANCE MARKETING

**Required Skills**

- Lead the Company's Growth Efforts for All Digital Marketing Departments
- A Track Record of 15 Years or More for Providing Hyper Growth for the Company
- Guide All Company Marketing Teams to Best-in-Class Results
- A Proven Data Guru
- Can Thrive in a High-Pressure Role

**Expected Salary: $150,000+**

The VP of Growth & Performance Marketing must be an inspirational leader who has already "been there and done that" in terms of building and inspiring high-performance teams at every level of their digital marketing career. This person's track record will speak for itself, showing capable of not just growth for the grand, but hyper growth. Often, the VP title requires 15 years or more of such a proven track record.

This career path is possible for the Director of SEM or display advertising who has provided this level of growth for the employer. However, it is likely that this person's SEM and/or display ad experience is just one facet of the newfound job responsibilities.

The new task is to guide the company's marketing teams toward best-in-class marketing results using all of the company's digital marketing strategies. Paid media marketing, inbound strategies, and more are all part of the VP's toolset, meaning the VP must be capable of overseeing SEM and display ad performance as well as SEO, website, and social media digital marketing growth.

Additionally, the VP is a data guru who is motivated by unlocking the secrets inherent in the data. The VP is always looking for ways to drive new channels to great success and finding ways to delight customers and target audiences reached by each marketing department. His or her ability to build relationships within the company is also used to develop relationships with company stakeholders and clients, using data analysis to communicate clear and well-defined business insights. The VP turns data into visualized goals and frameworks that can be used to guide the entire company toward positive business growth and outcomes.

This well-rounded position is not for the faint of heart, as the job demands and pressure are immense. For the driven digital marketer, resolve and dedication has already prepared them for success in this high-profile and prestigious role.

## SEARCH MARKETING IN THEORY VS. SEARCH MARKETING IN REALITY

So far in this book, I have stressed with some degree of regularity that adaptability and passion for the career is vital to success. A less talked about pillar of success is the importance of hard work. Yes, most people know that hard work is vital in almost any career path, but it is especially important to stress in the digital marketing world.

Many who are attracted by the possibilities of digital marketing are enticed by the glamorous and tech-savvy appeal of the industry. They think to themselves, "I'm ready make a name for myself in this exciting and growing career path." In all likelihood, they are ready to put in the hard work on strategizing and coming up with innovative ideas. That is wonderful, but are they equally as passionate about actually building those links? Talking strategy is exciting, but executing the strategy may not be as enticing to some.

Do not take this as a negative aspect of search marketing. Instead, treat it as someone who has been there giving you the honest truth. Search marketing in theory is awesome. It can even be awesome in practice. However, to truly excel, you will need to embrace the tedious nature of some elements of search marketing. Anyone who has spent seven hours straight doing something they do not like very much in pursuit of something they love will get the point. Whether you love cars, and spend all day under the hood tinkering and working up a sweat or love building custom PCs so you spend all day strategizing which parts fit best within the confines of your small form-factor PC, most hobbies, and passions conform to this rule.

In writing this book, it would be a mistake not to mention that the people who go furthest in this industry are willing to embrace the "not so exciting" to reap the rewards of this incredible field. Yes, SEM and display advertising are constantly evolving, providing the possibility of innovation and excitement at every turn, but the work itself can also be a pain in the butt.

For SEM, it is getting to see the results of your work as you watch a client's marketing efforts improve that makes the hard work worth it. Seeing the fruits of your labor make a difference in other people's lives is worth all the time and effort. That is why I am writing this book, after all. Additionally, if you are anything like me, that alone makes all the hard work worth it. That said, the stable career and healthy salaries do not hurt, either.

INTENTIONALLY LEFT BLANK

## 07

////////////////////////////////////////////////////

# EMAIL AGED LIKE FINE WINE, AND IT STILL HAS AN IMPORTANT PART TO PLAY IN THE FUTURE OF DIGITAL MARKETING

## WHAT YOU WILL LEARN IN THIS CHAPTER:

* Why the Death of Email Continues to Be Greatly Exaggerated
* Proven Email Marketing Best Practices That Drive Results
* Why Email Marketing Is the Average Consumer's Preferred Source of Direct Marketing
* What the Best Email Marketers Have in Common with Hall of Fame Coaches
* What Sets Email Marketers Apart from Other Digital Marketers

It seems like every year some so-called expert in the digital marketing space predicts the end of email marketing as we know it. Time and again, this notion is proved to be false. Email marketing is alive and well, and while it is no longer the new kid on the block, it still has much to offer the world of digital marketing.

A few statistics immediately invalidate the extreme overreaction of any claim about the death of email. First, worldwide email use continues to grow. An email statistics report conducted by The Radicati Group found that there were 2.6 billion email users worldwide in 2015. By 2019, the number of worldwide email users are expected to grow to 2.9 billion. Far from being a dying industry, email is actually a thriving industry. If The Radicati Group's forecast is accurate, more than one-third of the entire world's population will be using email by year's end in 2019.

Even better, the number of worldwide email accounts is projected to out-pace the growth of worldwide email users. What this means is that email users tend to have multiple email accounts. The reason for this is that many employees have a business/work-related account, and then they have a sepa-rate email accounts for personal correspondence or consumer-related email. As such, these consumer email accounts provide an incredible channel for brands to market products, specifically catering to a consumer email ac-count's desires, needs, and product preferences.

However, you may be like some of the experts who are skeptical of email marketing. Perhaps you think that email users are simply not all that active, making email marketing an inferior marketing tactic compared to a field like social media marketing. While this is a reasonable position to take at first glance, data reveals that 205 billion emails were sent and received per day in 2015. By 2019, that number is projected to move upwards of 246 billion emails. Consumers rely on emails for a few reasons. First, email is a conve-nient and accessible way to receive product updates and news about sales, which are always popular updates that consumers want to know. While con-sumer email may not be using email as a way to communicate with a brand in the same way as social media, it is a meaningful tool in a digital marketer's arsenal, particularly if the marketer is trying to sell products.

If you have an Amazon account, you are likely familiar with their targeted emails that let you know when a product in your Wish List has gone on sale. In all likelihood, you have sometimes clicked through to browse the website and take a second look at the product when you receive such emails.

Another great example of the power of email marketing in action comes by way of lifestyle brand Dormify, an eCommerce store that sells products designed for dorm rooms. Previously, Dormify used email marketing to just send out a blast email that was unfocused and untargeted. Dormify decided to switch over to automation instead, which automated three personalized messages for the following:

* A New Customer's "Welcome Email"
* A Personalized Email for When A Potential Customer Leaves an Item in the Cart
* A Personalized Post-Purchase Email

The end result of this three-fold approach toward personalized automation gave Dormify a 92% increase in email revenue, while its email audience converted at nearly double the rate of the site's average conversion.

This, in a nutshell, is the power of email marketing. 91% of email users check their email at least daily. The brands that provide influential email marketing will create a lasting effect on consumers when they check their email accounts.

Simply put, of all the digital marketing channels available, email marketing is arguably the best way to reach customers quickly and directly. How many marketing strategies give companies the ability to target consumers directly with a message that has a 91% chance of being seen on any given day? Framed in this way, it is easy to see why reports of the demise of email marketing are greatly exaggerated and wrong.

Still, there are right ways and wrong ways to go about email marketing. Simply bombarding a target list of potential customers is an awful way of representing a brand. Sending permission-based emails to customers who choose to opt-in to receiving newsletters and product updates via email, however, is a winning strategy. Not only do permission-based emailing tactics ensure you will not annoy people and harm your brand in the process, they also ensure you have a ready-made list of potential customers who have already indicated interest in your company and its products/message. In this way, a permission-based email campaign only grows a company's value.

In the words of industry influencer Seth Godin, earning permission is a "long-term profitable, scalable strategy that pays for itself." Godin contrasts the benefits of permission-based marketing with the harm a spam campaign of mass messaging will do to a brand. Godin notes that, while a spam campaign may feel like a smart idea, over time it devalues a brand and is the opposite of brand building. The best email marketing results stem from earning trust that comes from being honest about marketing communications and building a trusted relationship with the email account user. When a restaurant regularly relies on email discounts or a tech aficionado expects a weekly update on the latest electronics sale, it is likely that their trust was built from the ground up via an effective permission-based email campaign. Permission-based marketing refers to receiving a customer's permission to be solicited. In the context of email, permission-based marketing can be letting customers choose to enter their email address to sign up for a weekly or monthly newsletter.

Another essential element of effective email marketing is the visual component. Drab and forgettable emails that do nothing to attract a user's eyes will quickly be deleted or ignored. In a word, forgettable emails will be treated as forgettable. Thought and care needs to go into a successful email marketing campaign. Compelling visuals are a key element of a successful and thoughtful email campaign, and research proves this to be true.

Ninety percent of information transmitted to the brain is visual, and the brain processes visual information approximately 60,000 times faster than text-based information. Furthermore, 40% of people claim to respond better to a single image than 1,000 words. Now, quality text is still important in an email, to be sure, but the point is combining quality text with memorable visuals is an incredible combination for email marketing (or any marketing strategy, for that matter). However, you may well be wondering what quality visuals in an email campaign might look like.

Whether the email campaign utilizes beautiful infographics, a custom picture or an appealing video embedded within the email, the point is to stand out creatively and attract viewers. A natural extension of this general rule is that all visual content must be optimized for viewing on both mobile devices and desktops. Images that are too large will not play nicely with mobile, which is a critical error that can sabotage an email marketing campaign. According to Litmus Email Analytics, 55% of email is now opened on a mobile device, so any visual content absolutely must be optimized for mobile.

Car sharing service Uber nailed each of these elements in a 2016 targeted email campaign during St. Patrick's Day. Using a simple and clever visual with a green color scheme and four-leaf clover signifying the luck of the Irish, Uber immediately drew attention for its email campaign during a popular holiday. With the clever and simple image, Uber included a simple message: "Earn big on St. Patrick's Day - no luck needed." Uber sent out 179,000 of these messages and earned a 20% open rate for the holiday. That is a great way to drive user engagement and raise brand awareness by thinking outside the box with an innovative visually themed email strategy.

Additionally, when used effectively, email marketing campaigns can have a direct effect on the business's bottom line. In many respects, it is fair to call email marketing the king of conversions and ROI. eCommerce software firm Monetate found that 4.24% of email marketing visitors buy something, compared to a mere 2.49% among search engine visitors, and 0.59% of social media users. Even better, once you grow an email list with quality leads who opt-in to receive newsletters or sales updates, you own that list forever. In effect, you are talking about having a permanent, low-cost form of advertising that can serve as a constant conversion source, making it an indispensable marketing channel for the bottom line of many businesses.

The general rules of good email marketing are simple to understand, but skill and industry expertise is needed to master this form of marketing. The goals of email marketing, generally, are designed to accomplish the following:

* Use Direct Channel Marketing to Build and Maintain Customer Relationships
* Utilize the Cost-Effective Nature of Email Marketing to Directly Reach a Wide Audience
* Provide the Best ROI for a Brand's Marketing Efforts

Email marketing is here to stay because it is the best way for brands to speak to customers directly without breaking the bank. Effective email marketing provides one of the best ROI results for a brand since email marketing is low-cost but comes with big rewards. As such, skilled email marketers will always be in high demand.

# SKILLS NEEDED FOR A CAREER IN EMAIL MARKETING

Email marketing is desired to such an extent that a majority of companies surveyed by ExactTarget reported that they have a dedicated email marketing team (59% of the companies, to be exact). When skilled email marketing experts are staffed on a dedicated marketing team, email marketing becomes a powerful and persuasive tool used to achieve significant results via inexpensive marketing techniques.

With that said, smaller companies may not have an entire email marketing team, but rest assured that most companies still want to have an email list of prospective customers, even if an entire department is too expensive. These small organizations still look to hire experienced email marketers who can integrate and work effectively with other members of the marketing team. Simply put, email marketing skills are too valuable for even the smallest company to ignore if they are looking to expand in a meaningful way. Indeed, the low-cost nature of email marketing makes email marketers even more attractive to smaller companies with limited marketing budgets.

# MASTER PERMISSION-BASED MARKETING AND EMAIL ETIQUETTE

Since 2008, consumer desire to receive permission-based marketing through email has grown. Today, an incredible 74% of consumers prefer to receive permission-based marketing content via email. Compare this figure to the 5% who prefer permission-based text messaging and the 6% who prefer permission-based social channel marketing, and it is clear that permission-based marketing is where email dominates. Anyone looking for a long career as an email marketer must master permission-based marketing, if these trends hold. All indications are that these trends will hold and may even increase in the years ahead. Practicing email etiquette, then, is a key component of the successful email marketer. Knowing when to send an email is a critical skill to master.

## LEARN THE TOOLS OF MARKETING AUTOMATION AND CUSTOMER RELATIONSHIP MANAGEMENT

Still, just as important as permission-based marketing is marketing automation. Marketing automation is a subset of customer relationship management (CRM) focused on automating a marketing campaign's schedules, segmentation, tracking, and similar aspects of the campaign. Instead of relying on manual processes for these tasks, automation will make the campaign run more efficiently. Automation can be used to automatically send targeted, personalized messages to get a customer to opt-in to receive an email, for example. With marketing automation, individuals will opt-in to receive email, but they also will self-segment based on the individual's preferences or level of interaction. Simply put, marketing automation lets brands market automatically based on the decisions a customer makes. This allows the brand to provide different marketing content for every type of potential customer, making the marketing effort more targeted as a result. Platforms like Marketo, Infusionsoft, Ontraport and Drip are highly regarded solutions designed to help brands tap into the benefits of marketing automation.

One of the more important recent developments in email marketing is that employers are increasingly looking for employees who are familiar with customer resource management (CRM) software. As we just discussed, marketing automation is one extremely important subset of CRM, which highlights why familiarity with this software is so valued. In a broad sense, what is CRM?

This term simply refers to technology, software, and strategies a brand will use to manage and analyze customer interactions, data, and behaviors throughout their lifecycle as a customer. The reason CRM is essential from a marketing perspective is that there are many benefits of integrating a brand's email marketing and CRM efforts. For example, information gleaned from CRM customer insights can be used to create increasingly personalized email marketing campaigns. CRM can be used to synchronize names, dates, and similar data that will increase the relevance of the email to a reader. Increasing relevance in this way increases the likelihood an email will be opened and read, which is a cheap and effective way to use automation for improved email marketing results. Therefore, gaining experience with CRM platforms and software suites is an excellent way to stand out from fellow job applicants by providing expertise modern email marketing uses with increased regularity.

## MAINTAIN A FRESH, INTUITIVE APPROACH TO MARKETING EFFORTS TO KEEP EMAIL RECIPIENTS ENGAGED

Email marketers also need to have intuitive approaches to their marketing. While we have already discussed the fact that consumers are more willing to receive permission-based marketing via email, this reality is not a free pass for marketers to send redundant content. Email recipient fatigue is very real, and this can lead consumers to opt out from receiving a brand's emails. Few outcomes do more damage to a brand's reputation and ROI than losing valued customers who grew tired of the repetitive messaging. For this reason, email marketers are tasked with implementing fresh and innovative campaign ideas that continue to pique a consumer's interest in a meaningful way. Plainly, without excellent copywriting skills and valuable content, email consumers will look elsewhere to find more valuable content. An email marketer's job is to make sure the brand's content is always valuable and relevant.

## KNOW THE LAW TO STAY COMPLIANT

While this may come as a shock to you, email marketers need to remain aware of how anti-spam laws affect the business. Successful email marketers never expose their company to the risk of violating anti-spam laws. Companies with a global presence are particularly vulnerable since anti-spam laws differ by locality. Of course, quality email marketing never resorts to spam anyway, but it is worth reiterating that spam is not only annoying to consumers, but it can also get a business in legal trouble. These realities make it important for email marketers to know the difference between spam and quality permission-based content, and it may even open up unique job opportunities.

Some corporations and large companies forego having an in-house email marketing department because of strict spam laws. As a result, they need to outsource their email marketing needs to marketing agencies and similar providers with large staffs of trained email marketing experts. These experts must constantly be aware of the best practices and anti-spam laws around the world. This is a great career path for anyone with legal training as well as email marketing expertise or individuals who love law and digital marketing in nearly equal measure.

## HONE YOUR SKILL AS A COPYWRITER THAT PROVIDES VALUE-ADDS AND EFFECTIVE INCENTIVES

More than law, the most important skill an email marketer can possess is arguably strong copywriting skills. Since email marketing is largely a written word form of digital marketing via newsletters, sales letters and the like, strong command of the written word is a must. Compelling language that is at once persuasive and accessible creates a strong desire to open the emails and actually read them.

A good email marketer, however, does not only create compelling emails to send out. In addition, a good email marketer crafts a winning email list, but to do that, the marketer must create quality content that incentivizes people to give out their email address to receive said content. Startups and smaller blogs have adopted these tactics to great success.

If you are interested in experimenting with building your own email lists or venturing out as a successful email marketing entrepreneur, here are a few ideas to get you started. First, it is always a good idea to have an industry expert in your corner. To get quality advice on building your own email lists, opt-in to receive emails from an industry expert yourself. Check out Vero's blog to receive incredible email marketing advice and information you can use to enhance your knowledge of this thriving industry.

## TAKE THE TIME TO LEARN ABOUT SUCCESSES IN YOUR FIELD

Next, take a look at how others have succeeded on their startup journey. To use just one example of an inspiring startup success, let us take a look at Groove HQ and how they built an email list that was 100,000 subscribers strong. In their blog post celebrating the success, the first lesson Groove-

HQ imparts is that the blog's traffic strategy is also their email list strategy. Simply put, the more traffic that comes to the website, the more email list subscribers they will receive. To get people to come to their website, they embraced the UIU principle of content marketing. For anything they wrote, it had to be unique, interesting, and useful. This is a great strategy for building an email list since valuable content makes blog visitors need more of it. Finally, GrooveHQ advises bloggers hoping to build their own quality email list to find their own niche, reach out to influencers within that niche, and remain persistent and committed to building the email list.

While job skills are one thing, mere qualifications only suggest that a job applicant is qualified to perform essential job functions. A good, or even great, email marketer goes beyond mere qualifications and skillsets.

## WHAT MAKES A GOOD EMAIL MARKETER?

A good email marketer possesses a genuine interest and curiosity in the art of email marketing. Passion is essential in general when it comes to success in digital marketing, but it is perhaps most important in email marketing. Why? There is an extensive amount of testing in email marketing. In a word, email marketers are masters of A/B testing, which is the art of evaluating how a single change in an email message affects response rates, interactions, and click-through rates. Additional elements of an email message and/or campaign that must be tested and measured include varying subject lines, when messages are sent, the target audience segmentation, and visual/design elements of the message. Simply put, testing is a regular aspect of the job used to make key improvements.

In this way, email marketers need similar skills as a good coach. While job skills are well and good, the best coaches are the ones who "play the tapes back" and study what went wrong and what can be improved for the next game. Hall of fame level coaches are famous for their ability to study for hours and spend the sleepless nights needed to devise a winning strategy for the next game. In effect, the best coaches give their players the best chance to succeed. A skilled email marketer does the same thing for his or her email campaign and the client. Curiosity coupled with a self-starter's initiative are the qualities of a "hall of fame" email marketer, and if you master these qualities, you are well on your way to risking quickly in this industry.

Below are some of the job titles in the email marketing world that may provide insight on necessary job skills, expected salary, and possible career paths.

# EMAIL MARKETING COORDINATOR

### Required Skills
* Serve in a Supporting Role for Email Specialists and Senior Marketing Members
* Assist with Campaign Production by Making Sure That Email Links and Personalized Fields Work as Needed
* Perform Tests to Ensure a Consistent User Experience for All Major Browsers and Email Platforms
* Check Email Campaign Quality by Proofreading for Typos, Grammatical Errors and Template Mistakes
* Be a Team Player Who Treats the Support Role Seriously

**Expected Salary: $35,000 to $45,000**

The role of email marketing coordinator is an excellent entry-level position for learning how email marketing campaigns are successfully strategized, produced, and executed. A coordinator is expected to serve a supporting role to the specialist for a wide variety of marketing tasks.

Ordinarily, this person assists the specialists and senior marketing team members with production work for an email campaign, which may involve confirming that all email links, dynamic content, and personalized fields are functioning as intended. Similarly, expect to test for a consistent user experience across all major internet browsers and email platforms.

Depending on the size of the company and email department, coordinators may also be expected to help with promotion management for the email campaign. If so, the coordinator should be capable of helping with print production and proofreading to make sure emails and messages have the proper spelling, grammar, form, and template.

Treat this support role seriously, and it can serve as valuable experience that becomes your launching pad to an email marketing specialist promotion.

# EMAIL MARKETING SPECIALIST

### Required Skills

- Building Email Campaigns and Measuring the Results
- Perform Day-to-Day Email Marketing Activities Such as Email Campaign Setup and Testing
- Be Up-to-Date on the Latest Email Marketing Best Practices
- Troubleshooting Skills to Solve Any Issues Harming an Email Campaign's Execution
- The Ability to Code, Design, and Test Email Campaigns Effectively

### Expected Salary: $45,000 to $55,000

The email marketing specialist is a marketing pro responsible for day-to-day execution of the company's email marketing programs. As such, this position is a critical component of how businesses meet their marketing objectives. Without specialists who set up, maintain, and review email marketing campaigns and communications, businesses lack the insight needed to improve performance.

Achieving these job expectations requires specialists to understand the latest email marketing best practices so they can be applied to executing a professional campaign that delivers a substantial ROI. With this job title comes the expectation that the employee will stay constantly up to date on the latest email marketing standards. This knowledge empowers the email marketing specialist to design and test the email campaign with greater efficiency that leads to meaningful improvement.

# EMAIL MARKETING MANAGER

### Required Skills

- Provide a Detailed Plan of Action to Achieve a Brand's Email Marketing Goals
- Managing the Email List of Target Users/Consumers
- Managing Creative Development within an Email Marketing Department
- Ensuring All Policies and Email Campaigns Comply with Anti-Spam Laws
- See How Team Is Performing A/B Testing

### Expected Salary: $70,000 to $90,000

As the primary position career email marketers aspire to achieve, this position is tasked with developing, executing, and effectively tracking email marketing campaigns/programs. The overarching goal of the email marketing manager is to help a company fulfill its strategies of obtaining and retaining customers, with email marketing as the means to those ends.

Email marketing managers at larger organizations coordinate with email marketing specialists and analysts who assist the email marketing manager in meeting marketing goals and tasks. Managers must create overarching strategies to achieve company goals and ensure employees are staying on message and on target. Overseeing the work product of all employees is a necessity to maintain quality oversight of campaigns while also protecting the brand from running afoul of any anti-spam laws. Additionally, if the company works with outside vendors, the email marketing manager must coordinate with them to develop a cohesive and consistent marketing vision.

Like all email marketers, the manager must also oversee the team's A/B testing while also analyzing email campaign performances to ensure the team is operating efficiently. Where the manager differs from an email marketing specialist, however, is that he or she must offer recommendations pertaining to campaign improvements to marketing decision makers within the company.

Finally, the manager also works to ensure that schedules and project deadlines are met, while generating new contact sources who opt-in to receiving the brand's email marketing messages. Part of ensuring the company performs as needed is by setting key performance indicators (KPIs), benchmarks for gauging whether department goals are met. The manager oversees and reviews KPI performance to ensure the team is staying on track.

## DIRECTOR OF EMAIL MARKETING ★★★★

**Required Skills**

- Establish a Successful Career Built on Delivering Effective Email Marketing Campaigns
- Oversee All Email Marketing Development, Implementation and Optimization Strategies
- Identify, Create and Optimize Relevant Offers That Entice Readers in a Campaign

- Be Capable of Improving the Company's Reputation Through Email Marketing
- Regularly Report Campaign Results to Top Executives

**Expected Salary: $90,000 to $105,000**

Make a career of continuously delivering successful and effective email marketing campaigns, and you will be well on your way toward heading the entire department. Such responsibility is precisely what awaits the Director of Email Marketing.

The responsibilities afforded to this executive give the director immense influence in determining overall company success. The big picture of the director's responsibility requires oversight of the entire email marketing department, meaning the director is responsible for all email marketing development, implementation, and optimization strategies. Realistically, this means millions of members across the company's websites and email activities can be directly affected by what strategies the director chooses to take.

The director must also oversee mailing schedules, all while identifying, creating and optimizing relevant email marketing offers that entice readers. All job functions of the director are meant to maximize the company's reputation through email marketing, which may require regular reporting of campaign results to the Vice President of Email Marketing or the company President.

## VP OF EMAIL MARKETING

**Required Skills**

- Guide the Entire Email Marketing Department Through All Phases of Email Marketing
- Create Fresh Marketing Campaign Ideas that Continue to Innovate
- Attract Customers at Every Stage of the Customer Lifecycle
- Have the Ability to Multitask and Shift Marketing Focus on the Fly
- Possess the Intuitive Ability to Deliver the Right Marketing Messages at the Right Moments

**Expected Salary: $120,000 to $150,000**

Rise to the top of the email marketing ladder, and a position as VP of Email Marketing is the reward for years of hard work. The VP guides the Director of Email Marketing and the entire department through every key phase of the email marketing, from the planning stage to execution.

The VP has built a career on creating fresh email marketing campaign ideas and recommendations that filter down to the rest of the department. As such, the VP frequently collaborates with the company's creative and content teams to develop sophisticated communication systems designed to attract customers at every stage of the customer lifecycle.

As we have discussed in this chapter, the best way to target customers is to provide marketing content that speaks to them specifically. The VP understands this, creating systems designed to provide tailored marketing that can shift its focus depending on the customer in question. Existing customers will receive marketing focused on retention, whereas potential customers will receive marketing content prioritizing awareness or engagement.

One of the best ways to achieve these goals is by prioritizing marketing automation as part of the brand's customer relationship management (CRM) efforts. The VP plays a chief role overseeing these efforts, such as retargeting and similar automation initiatives. Why? For starters, the bottom line of the business can benefit significantly from automation and CRM. Recent data from 2016 reveals that better email marketing is one of the primary benefits for companies that have embraced automation.

VPs love email marketing because they have spent their entire career delivering the right message with the right offer at precisely the right moment. This is what the VP continues to do on a broad organizational scale, which makes this job such a rewarding position after years of digital and email marketing excellence.

## WHAT SETS A CAREER IN EMAIL MARKETING APART

For starters, email marketers must be comfortable and familiar with handling personally identifiable information. Marketing professionals need to know how to treat sensitive information of this nature with the discretion and safety best practices they deserve. Email marketing pros need to know how to transfer or share this information in a safe manner without compromising consumer safety and security. If email marketing teams fail to do this, an entire brand's reputation could be harmed.

Email professionals are also more aware than most of the effect mistakes can have on job performance. In other fields of digital marketing, a campaign error may be easily fixed or remedied without a great deal of harm being done. Not so, however, in email marketing. The popular phrase that "emails are forever" holds true for marketers. The lesson? Experience in email marketing will increase your eye for quality, and like a good lawyer, you will look at marketing content carefully to avoid any non-fixable mistakes.

Finally, email marketers gain a unique appreciation for how consumers and potential customers are turned into actual customers. In other words, email marketers learn key insights into the full conversion path of an end user. Leading email clients such as Gmail and Yahoo offer unique features and capabilities for sending creative emails. Similarly, each browser (Chrome, Firefox, and Safari) may affect how a message is read. Each of these affects the user experience, and just one little tweak from A/B testing can increase conversion by 20% or much more, as a wealth of case studies have proven. As technology continues to shape which devices can be used as addressable marketing opportunities (from smartphones to smartwatches), email marketers will be ready to react. Their career opportunities have already prepared them to look at how to tweak marketing efforts based on the ways an end user will react to content depending on how they consume it.

In these ways and so many more, email is not dead. Nor is it a dying breed that is living on borrowed time. Email marketing is yet another exciting component of digital marketing's bright and promising future.

INTENTIONALLY LEFT BLANK

08

# MAKING THE PITCH FOR A CAREER IN DIGITAL MARKETING SALES

## WHAT YOU WILL LEARN IN THIS CHAPTER:

* Why Digital Sales is a Central Component of Digital Marketing
* How a Single Blog and a Sales Team Added Tens of Millions in Value to Their Company
* "The Law of 250" That Leads to Sustained Sales Success
* Actionable Tips to Make You a Better Salesperson

For almost any business, sales are the lifeblood that allows a business to thrive. When nothing gets sold, a business cannot succeed, simple as that. Digital marketing is no exception to this rule since it is still a business, after all. When digital brands fail to provide an effective sales pitch, the reality is these brands will lag behind their competitors.

While the world of digital marketing has changed a great many things related to how brands do business, sales is relatively unchanged in one key respect. Even in today's increasingly digital world, effective sales and eCommerce requires a deft human touch and a strong sense of people skills.

Of course, digital marketing sales does rely on technical savvy that a door-to-door or brick and mortar salesperson would not need, but the general rule is the same. If you are outgoing, personable and are not afraid of rejection, a career in digital marketing sales will be a rewarding endeavor.

A career in digital marketing sales may task you with selling physical products through a brand's various eCommerce channels, but it is also increasingly likely that you could be selling entirely digital goods via digital marketing. For example, take a look at the music streaming business. In the music industry, for example, the global revenue of digital music alone is nearing $7 billion. Then, consider other popular entertainment platforms such as Steam, the most popular platform for digital PC games. Valve—the company which owns the Steam distribution service—is a household name for gamers, but it may come as a shock that Valve's distribution service has sold more than 350 million copies of digital games, generating the company just under $3.5 billion in earnings for 2016 alone.

As digital sales continue to grow, rest assured that digital marketing is still more needed than ever for selling physical products as well. Indeed, effective digital marketing can make all the difference for a brand's sales results for their physical products. Deloitte estimates that digital technologies influenced 49% of in-store sales, an estimated $1.7 trillion. In short, even when digital sales efforts do not lead to an online sale, it is quite likely that the effort will be rewarded at brick and mortar storefronts. Sometimes, all it takes to reap big rewards is one blog, a winning strategy, and a dedicated sales team.

## AT&T COMBINED A BLOG, A GREAT SALES TEAM AND A WINNING STRATEGY TO CREATE SALES SUCCESS

In late 2011, Sander Biehn's employer, AT&T, put together a new sales team to rebuild relationships with a former customer and Fortune 100 company in Atlanta. To achieve this goal, the team decided to take on a new approach. Namely, they wanted to build relationships via social media since the company was forced to try something new. Sales had dried up, and the relationship between the companies had soured as a result.

To fix the problem, the team reached out to renowned industry influencer Mark Schaefer. With Mark's training and support from the internal sales team, AT&T devised a content strategy targeting strategic people of interest from their former customer. The goal was to create new discussion opportunities on social media, far removed from the heated passions and disconnect between the companies. Eighteen months later, AT&T received $47 million in new business thanks to their social media outreach and social sales strategy. Here is how AT&T made it happen.

AT&T knew it would need to create compelling content that offered its former customer valuable information and solutions to their business. The sales team looked at AT&T's solutions to the former customer's problems, and it found 10 such solutions that they could teach customers about in a helpful way. The means of providing this valuable information was AT&T's blog, called Networking Exchange, but putting this quality content out there on their blog was not enough. AT&T also needed to build an audience comprised of "people of interest" that would view the information. To achieve this, AT&T leveraged LinkedIn and Twitter to broadcast their marketing message.

Long story short, AT&T's approach of using social media and quality content made AT&T a thought leader who was authentically respected in this sphere of industry. In the end, AT&T's authentically helpful approach to customer engagement led to bid requests for projects, helping thaw those formerly icy relationships. Within 18 months AT&T's blog and content strategy led to $47 million in new business, all of which was directed at the 10 solutions their sales team had identified from the first day.

This case study aptly describes the power of digital marketing sales in a nutshell. Developing a sales strategy is a core component of what a digital marketing sales team will do for large brands, and then the team will incorporate and execute a strategy that transforms the goal of increased sales into a reality.

Are you unsure whether digital marketing sales is the right path for you?

Well, in truth, a career in any kind of sales, digital marketing, or otherwise, is not for everyone. You will need a thick skin, commitment, and relentless tenacity. It is commonly known that turnover in regular sales jobs is quite high. Digital marketing sales is no exception. Digital marketing salespeople are constantly under pressure to perform, meaning that generating business is a constant must. If business is not being generated as a result of a salesperson's efforts, they may be shown the door in short order.

Regardless, the sky is the limit for a successful salesperson, and best of all, there are little to no educational or work history barriers. If you have the intuition, people skills, and digital savvy to make a company money by way of sales, you will be highly sought after. Best of all, there are fewer limitations on your earning potential. Like regular sales jobs, plenty of digital sales roles rely on commissions and similar incentives that produce big earning opportunities for the best digital salespeople.

The best salespeople will not be turned away by the high turnover rates and competitive atmosphere. Instead, they embrace it and use those challenges as fuel to rise to the top of the sales world, all while reaping significant benefits of being a renowned salesperson.

## SKILLS NEEDED FOR DIGITAL MARKETING SALES SUCCESS

If someone has ever convinced you to buy a product you had no intention of buying previously, you have experienced skillful sales traits firsthand. Recall a time when a product you did not even know you needed transformed into a product you could not do without because of the way it was marketed to you. In all likelihood, you made an impulse buy after the salesperson was finished working their magic.

While the sale may have seemed spontaneous to you, it was no accident when viewed through the eyes of the effective salesperson. Sales, after all, is a highly measurable process. Here are the traits needed to succeed in this field.

## LEVERAGING DATA AND RESILIENCE TO DRIVE SALES

Sales representatives often know exactly who to call and how many sales presentations are needed to close a deal. This is especially true in the digital world, thanks to the treasure troves of data that brands can tap into. Despite these benefits, it is harder to get a "yes" from a customer than you think. How many times has a sales pitch failed to work on you? In all likelihood, you have rejected more sales pitches than you have accepted.

As such, a salesperson needs tenacity first and foremost. That is the only way to consistently turn a "no" into a "yes." Whether marketing to another business or to a customer, a digital marketing sales professional should expect initial resistance to the sale. This is unsurprising, considering that salespeople are actively trying to part businesses and customers from their money. A customer must feel valued and that the product itself is valuable for a salesperson to achieve sustainable and repeatable success. The best salespeople learn to adapt when hearing "no" for an answer.

## RESILIENCE NEEDS TO BE PAIRED WITH GENUINE EMPATHY

The first trait that turns a "no" into a regular "yes" is empathy. Rather than being a pushy "snakeoil" salesman simply looking to sell a product at any cost, the digital salesperson must be empathic and capable of listening. In digital sales, a marketing manager is often responsible for passing over warm leads, which are potential customers who have shown interest in the company or its products. These leads are passed to the salesperson, who is tasked with the responsibility of closing the sale. This is why empathy and listening skills are crucial. A salesperson must be acutely aware of the customer's needs, desires, and wants in order to convert expressed interest into a sale.

## ELIMINATING DISTRACTIONS IS ESSENTIAL

Another corollary trait of the successful salesperson is focus. If sales is not something you are passionate about and wholeheartedly focused on, that apathy will come through in digital sales efforts. Distractions about in 21st century living, whether you are the customer or the salesperson. Cutting through that noise and grabbing a potential customer's focused attention is critical for sales success, and achieving this in a crowded market comes via focus. What do we mean by focus? For one, you must know the product you are selling and to whom it is being sold. Second, you must put all your effort into selling the product effectively via the many channels of digital marketing. Leveraging social media, email, eCommerce, mobile, or all of the above will ensure you make the most out of your digital sales efforts.

Sometimes, however, even the most focused sales pitches will not lead to an immediate yes. Imagine, for example, you are in the market for new online software and come across a particularly enticing sales pitch. You head over to the brand's website, like what you see, but you just do not have enough incentive to make the purchase. Perhaps you opt-out of purchasing because of budgetary reasons, or maybe it is simply because the product is new and you are a buyer who waits for more feedback from reputable sources in the software industry. For this reason, a salesperson needs tenacity and commitment to complete the sale. Just because the first sales pitch does not lead to a sale, the focused salesperson does not give up on figuring out a way to close the deal.

## UTILIZE PROVEN DIGITAL MARKETING STRATEGIES TO HELP MAKE THE SALE AND IMPROVE PRODUCTS

This is where the "digital marketing" side of digital sales comes into play. The internet has changed the game for businesses by providing access to a global audience, but that global audience comes with increased competition. As such, the digital salesperson needs a strong digital sales strategy to make the most of sales efforts. Whether you are an entrepreneur in business for yourself or part of a digital sales team—complete with C-suite executives, managers, and department heads—you need a committed strategy to making the most of digital sales opportunities.

## POUR YOUR TENACITY AND COMMITMENT INTO A THREE-FOLD APPROACH FOCUSING ON THE FOLLOWING:

* Promotions/Marketing: How do you describe the product, help it gain visi-

bility, and make it appealing?

* Product Delivery: Ask whether payments are securely processed and whether customers receive prompt delivery of purchased goods. Simply, are they getting great customer service?
* Product Perfection: Feedback from the sales team should be used to improve existing products.

It is impossible for customers to buy a product they do not know exists. This is why promotions and marketing are a crucial component of digital sales efforts. Digital sales managers and executives are tasked with formulating the plans a digital sales team will execute, and the plans are often wide-reaching. Utilizing social media platforms, affiliate marketing and other prominent digital marketing channels will go a long way toward raising awareness for your products, thereby helping sales reps seal the deal.

Second, product delivery is another essential element of successful sales. This form of "content delivery," however, is not focused on content in the typical sense of the word for marketing purposes. Here, we are not referring to blog content or similar value-adding content, but rather to the way products are delivered. Once a marketing strategy has paid off, salespeople will start generating sales, leading to added revenue. Additionally, salespeople are tasked with selling and closing deals when they receive inquiries about certain products. Successful salespeople turn these leads and inquiries into a steady stream of customers. However, digital marketing sales is about more than just getting a customer. You also must make sure customers are happy, and how products are delivered plays a key role in this regard. A digital sales team tackles challenges pertaining to prompt product delivery, secure processing of online payments, and similar strategies that lead to exemplary customer service.

Finally, for large and small brands alike, products must be improved from time to time. The sales team can play a meaningful role in this refining process. When trying to make sales, representatives will frequently hear feedback from customers. Some of this feedback could provide:

* Reasons Why the Product Is Not Something the Customer Wants to Buy
* Tangible Ways the Product Could Be Improved in the Future
* Whether the Price Point Is Ideal

# ABOVE ALL, LEARN TO LISTEN

Taking these factors into account, it is clear that a skilled salesperson must be a good listener. A sales rep will need to have a firm grasp on what the brand is selling, in order to convey the precise reasons that a product is desirable. The best sales reps can expect to be asked what customers are telling them when sales efforts are made. Asking the right questions and listening to the answers requires a focused and attentive rep with a clear understanding of the brand's products and the customers they serve.

# MAKING A NAME FOR YOURSELF IN DIGITAL SALES

People are wise enough to pick up on the fact you are only in it for you. That is not the recipe for a successful digital marketing sales career. As such, you must strike the right balance between striving to achieve your goals and working to meet the needs of your sales prospects. Legendary salesperson Joe Girard's "Law of 250" demonstrates why meeting the needs of sales prospects is so essential.

Before he ever sold more vehicles than 95% of all North American car dealers—incredibly, he sold them all at retail, one car at a time—Girard attended a funeral that would change his life and outlook on sales forever. The funeral Girard attended was Catholic, so Mass cards were given out to all in attendance. Girard asked the funeral director how he knew the precise number of Mass cards to print. The director informed Girard the number of funeral attendees almost always averages out to about 250. Thus, the funeral director prints 250 for each and every funeral.

Soon after attending this funeral, Girard sold a vehicle to a Protestant funeral director. Recalling the 250 lesson he learned from the Catholic funeral director, Girard inquired how many individuals attend a Protestant funeral on average. Again, he received the same answer: 250. He then attended a wedding, and asked the same question to the minister. The answer? About 250 on the bride's side and an additional 250 on the groom's side.

Girard used this empirical data to devise his so-called "Law of 250." The basic principle of Girard's law is that most individuals have approximately 250 people who would show up to their wedding or funeral. He used this information in a few meaningful ways. First, he understood that if he did an awful job of understanding his sales prospects or sold them a terrible product, he may well lose 250 more customers. Regardless, there is a positive angle. If he did an incredible job, he stood to gain 250 customers.

With this general understanding, he then aimed to gain referrals and build his business by focusing on three factors within his control. First, he called a customer within a few weeks of selling the car, making sure the car was running well. If the customer was satisfied, he would ask for a referral then. If something was wrong, he would fix the issue before requesting a referral.

Next, he kept a file of his customer's personal information. This includes things like birthdays, their occupation, and even more obscure information like the birthdays of their kids. With this information written down, he would use it to make conversations warm and personalized in a way they would not have been otherwise. Making people feel special, important, and remembered is a great way to build business, whether you are selling cars or pursing a digital marketing career.

Finally, Girard sent a greeting card once a month to every customer on his list without fail. Girard intuitively understood the importance of brand consistency, constantly reminding customers he was a business person who cared. Girard understood above all else that so long as he built strong relationships with customers and valued them, his job as a salesperson would be easier in the long run. Go the extra mile for your customers, and make sure they have a full picture of the products your employer provides. In this way, you will make it easier on yourself to achieve your sales goals, while also meaningfully improving the lives of those who buy what you are selling.

If you are excited to make a name for yourself and better the lives of customers, here are a few of the thrilling opportunities in digital sales.

# DIGITAL MEDIA SALES SPECIALIST

**Required Skills**
- Can Thrive on Understanding What Businesses Need to Create Custom Solutions that Meet Those Needs
- Be a Self-Motivated, Goal-Driven Employee
- Stay Current on Digital Media Developments
- Work With Account Executives to Coordinate Marketing, Advertising and Promotional Activities
- Diligently Work to Meet Daily, Weekly, and Monthly Sales Goals

**Expected Salary: $35,000 to $55,000**

This entry-level role is a natural fit for the aspiring digital marketer who thrives on creativity and understanding what businesses need before making the sale. While a sales specialist is an entry-level title, the person in this role is given significant responsibility from the outset once trained, working directly with clients and businesses to understand their needs.

Once the specialist assesses the business and their needs, he or she uses creativity and digital marketing experience to create custom solutions that are designed to meet those business needs.

In addition to making sales, the specialist is also relied upon for working with account executives to coordinate marketing, advertising, and promotional activities/opportunities. This should not necessarily come as a surprise since these efforts can be crucial toward making sales.

No matter what is being sold by the brand (apps, services, or products), the specialist should stay current on the latest developments in digital media. The latest industry evolutions are sure to become important for the specialist, particularly if they wish to earn a promotion with greater authority and responsibility.

Most importantly, sales managers and bosses give the specialist daily, weekly, and monthly sales goals to meet. For this reason, the specialist should be a diligent self-starter who is capable of keeping motivated for the long haul to meet long-term sales goals. If a specialist establishes a reputation for being a leading salesperson, promotions are sure to follow in short order.

## DIGITAL MEDIA SALES EXECUTIVE

### Required Skills

* Develop Strong Relationships with the Clients You Serve
* Drive Results for Clients by Collaborating with Internal Sales and Marketing Teams
* Develop Strategic Plans Focused on Customer Understanding, Relationship Building, and Driving Revenue
* Implement Strategies That Work Within the Confines of the Larger Company Vision Outlined by the Manager or Director
* Balance Creativity and Innovation with the Desire to Be a Team Player

### Expected Salary: $60,000 to $70,000

Executives will likely be charged with developing strong relationships with decision makers, executives with other companies and new clients. Similarly, they may even be tasked with specific accounts. In this way, executives can be seen as specialists of sorts who must build strategic plans for clients.

To that end, executives must demonstrate that, over their years of digital sales experience, they have a strong focus on customer understanding, relationship building, and driving revenue. For these reasons, you can see why the skills we have talked about in this chapter can be used as a platform to leap to prominent executive positions.

While focused on clients, the executive must also collaborate with internal team to create more effective sales efforts and drive results for clients. This is a position, as you may have guessed, that is available in companies that obtain sales by serving the needs of large clients. While executives are tasked with developing strategic plans as mentioned, it is important to understand they develop these plans within the confines of overall marketing strategies and campaign ideas that are passed down by their manager or director. There is a great degree of creative flexibility for the executive, so long as their strategy adheres to the larger vision and guidelines laid out by bosses.

For this reason, to succeed in this sales position, it is important to be both a creative visionary and a team player. Manage this balance effectively, and it may not be long before the sales executive has earned a promotion to Digital

Marketing Sales Manager.

## DIGITAL MARKETING SALES MANAGER

### Required Skills

- Creating a Positive Sales Culture and Comprehensive Vision for the Sales Team
- Capable of Conceptualizing and Designing Winning Sales Strategies
- The Ability to Work Effectively and Coordinate with Other Departments
- Creativity and Strong Communication Skills Are a Must for This Important Managerial Position

### Expected Salary: $70,000 to $90,000

An integral part of the sales management team, the Digital Sales Manager is tasked with creating a positive culture focused on delivering sales results. While sales reps are tasked primarily with selling, the sales manager must be a creative thinker capable of conceptualizing and producing sales strategies that generate leads and results.

This managerial position must work in tandem with other digital marketing departments (such as advertising and social media marketing departments) in order to form a comprehensive digital sales plan that translates into an effective company vision. Quick thinking creativity is essential, as well as a thick skin. Sales managers must be able to sell up and down, and they must even be capable of selling ideas to top brass when marketing and sales goals conflict.

This is a great stepping stone for quality sales reps who are ready for a more stable form of employment with predictable hours and quality benefits.

# DIGITAL MEDIA SALES DIRECTOR

### Required Skills
* Expert Knowledge of Digital Sales
* Lead the Entire Company's Digital Sales Efforts
* Coordinate with Internal Sales Teams, Marketing, C-Suite Executives, Product Design Teams and More
* A Proven Track Record Capable of Opening Doors to New Customers
* The Ability to Develop Strong Relationships with Customers and Company Executives

### Expected Salary: $120,000 to 140,000

For those who work their way up the ladder to Digital Sales Director, the buck stops with you in terms of the company's digital sales efforts. As a result, you will be working directly with internal digital sales teams, marketing departments, C-Suite execs, product design teams, and engineering (assuming the business creates physical products as well).

The company's goals of revenue and sales increases are your burden to accomplish, so these professionals must thrive in a high-pressure environment where company success rests in no small part on the sales director's capable shoulders. This position needs to develop strong relationships with customers and internal executives alike since this title requires balancing the understanding of company goals and a customer or client's needs.

Directors thrive as a brand's most experienced seller, using that experience to inspire the rest of the team to tell the brand's story in the most effective way. Directors, then, are more than just effective team leaders, although they are certainly that as well.

They are master salespeople who understand what customers need, using their years of experience to motivate and mobilize the customer base. They must also have a strong grasp of analytics, matching their masterful sales instinct with the digital marketing knowledge needed to bring creative and data-driven solutions to the sales team.

# VP OF DIGITAL ADVERTISING

## Required Skills
- Takes Responsibility for the Company's Sales and Digital Marketing Sales Centers
- Oversee a Brand's Paid Digital Media, CRM Software and Consumer/B2B Partnerships that Affect Sales Results
- Creates and Manages the Sales Department Budget and Calendar
- Always Looks for Ways to Improve KPI's and Make Sales Efforts More Efficient and Diverse
- Constantly Seek New and Emerging Channels That Can Bring New Customers, Marketing Opportunities or Revenue Streams

**Expected Salary: $130,00+**

Succeed in digital marketing sales efforts, and you may well be entrusted with the esteemed position of VP of Digital Advertising.

A VP of Digital Advertising is responsible for the results of a company's sales and digital marketing media sales teams and centers, and additional responsibilities may stem from this primary duty. For example, it is not uncommon for a VP in this role to also be responsible for the brand's paid digital media, customer resource management software and consumer/business to business (B2B partnerships), since digital media sales may heavily rely on these additional tools and resources.

Also expect to oversee strategic and logistical aspects of the brand's marketing efforts, such as being responsible for the digital sales budget and managing the sales department's calendar, analytics strategies, and profit reports.

The successful VP is always looking for ways to improve KPI's of scale, making the brand's sales effort more efficient, while also seeking to appeal to a broader and more diverse customer base.

The diverse nature of the VP's daily duties ensures that he or she must constantly seek out new or emerging channels that might provide new customer opportunities, marketing opportunities or revenue streams.

# THE ENTREPRENEURIAL PATH TOWARD DIGITAL SALES

While much of this chapter has focused on digital sales roles within companies and digital marketing departments, do not be afraid to go it alone in an entrepreneurial venture. There is not a single entrepreneur in existence that could not benefit from just a bit of extra motivation and/or inspiration.

To that end, let's finish this chapter with an inspirational example of the entrepreneurial spirit within the world of digital sales. Gary Vaynerchuk is now a household name in the tech and startup world, but his unlikely rise to fame and success came from an inventive entrepreneurial venture.

While Vaynerchuk is known today as a renowned entrepreneur and New York Times best-selling author, his entrepreneurial spirit existed long before the fame came to his doorstep. After finishing his freshman year of college, Vaynerchuk went back home for a spell, where he worked at his dad's liquor shop in New Jersey. The year was 1994, a time when internet business was a largely untapped phenomenon. Still, Vaynerchuk saw an opportunity. Namely, he thought there was a market for the first ever wine eCommerce business.

According to Vaynerchuk, he did not see the need for 8,000 physical stores. He realized a simple online storefront would suffice. Three years after this epiphany, WineLibrary.com was launched. Like any entrepreneur, Gary learned about the tools he would need to succeed, such as Google AdWords. Over time, he grew his dad's store from an annual revenue of $3 million to $45 million by 2003. From there, Vaynerchuk kept selling, all while staying in touch with his followers and brand message.

Through a simple webcast, he commanded the attention of thousands of wine enthusiasts, and this success grew to become Wine Library TV—a web video series where Vaynerchuk tasted and discussed all things wine. His hammed up antics and wild gesticulations quickly made him a viral sensation. In other words, he knew his audience, what they were looking for, and never looked back.

What is Gary's advice for those who would like to succeed in digital marketing and the world of sales as he did? Two words: be authentic. According to Vaynerchuk, if he does not feel good about what he is selling, he is dead. While perhaps a bit of an exaggeration, the simple point remains. To make it as a salesperson, whether as an entrepreneur or company sales rep, you need to love what you do.

While some view selling a product as pretending to care, Gary's secret is that his success as a salesman is owed to the fact he actually does care. People have no interest in being scammed by a snake-oil salesman. Instead, they want genuine help to receive products that make a meaningful difference in their lives. Adopt this mindset and embrace authenticity and a constant learning attitude. Remain a constant listener who is focused on your goals as a salesperson and your customer's needs. Do this, and success will come in short order.

INTENTIONALLY LEFT BLANK

# 09

# SEO CONTINUES TO BE A SPRINGBOARD INTO THE WORLD OF DIGITAL MARKETING

→

---

## WHAT YOU WILL LEARN IN THIS CHAPTER:

* Why Adaptability is Essential to the Industry of SEO and Your Career in the Field
* Why the Death of SEO is an Outright Falsehood as the Demand for SEO Grows
* How to Take Advantage of SEO's Continuous Changes
* How SEO Is Leveraged with Other Forms of Digital Marketing to Maximize Results
* What Career Paths Are Available When Pursuing SEO
* How Persistence Will Be the Story Behind Your SEO Success

Evolutionary theorist Charles Darwin once uttered famous words on the important role adaptability plays with regards to evolution. According to Darwin's *Origin of Species*, "it is not the most intellectual of the species that survives; it is not the strongest that survives; but the species that survives is the one that is able best to adapt and adjust to the changing environment in which it finds itself." Replace species with "digital marketing professional," and Darwin may as well have been talking about a career in search engine optimization (SEO). Simply put, the ever-changing nature of SEO means that the successful professional is adaptable.

To explain why adaptability is one of several skills you will need to thrive in the world of SEO, one must know what SEO is as a practical matter. In plain English, SEO is simply activity undertaken to improve search engine rankings. Unlike PPC's paid search via Google Adwords, there is no payment involved with SEO. Instead, SEO is the process of gaining increased traffic and visibility simply by using organic and free marketing efforts to rank higher in search engines. To understand the importance of SEO, consider your experiences browsing search results on Google.

Organic link building is important because it is one of the most important ways to get backlinks to a website or blog. Backlinks, for reference, are links on one website that, when clicked, take the user to a separate website. If you use the internet, you are already familiar with backlinks. Imagine reading a news report covering a new business, and there is a link to said business's website. If you click on it, you have just clicked on a backlink. An organic link, then, is a link from somebody else's website or blog that links to your website without being asked to do so. From Google's perspective, this shows your website content is eminently relevant, authoritative, and shareable when enough people organically link to your website.

Google will display links to pages that it considers most relevant and/or authoritative for a given search. In the early years of Google's SEO algorithms, shoddy tactics like keyword stuffing and "black-hat" linking schemes were rewarded. Ever since Google implemented its so-called Penguin algorithm in 2012, Google has aggressively targeted these linking schemes and keyword stuffing practices. This was Google's first game-changing foray into encouraging quality content and organic backlinking to gain better search engine results. In the years that followed, it became clear that content was king.

This oft-mentioned refrain of "content is king" simply means that providing valuable, informative, and engaging content is an essential step toward improving search rankings. Why is content so important? When content is valuable, it gets linked by other blogs. This leads to helping a brand generate links, which is a significant factor in search engine rankings. To put this concretely, Google displays links to pages that it considers both relevant and authoritative. Google algorithms make this determination largely on the basis of both the number and quality of links from other pages on the web. Boiled down to the essence of SEO, a brand's webpages can rank highly in Google so long as other pages link to them.

Practically speaking, clever title tags, using the right keywords for short URL slugs, and choosing the right content length will all affect rankings in meaningful ways. While these tactics are beyond the scope of this book, know that over time, Google's algorithms will recognize these as proof that the content is authoritative and relevant. In the process, so long as quality content continues to be created and shared, a brand can enjoy strong Google ranking results that are sustainable.

There are many tactics used to make link building as successful as it is, and Moz covers a number of these in his excellent *Beginner's Guide to Link Building*. For example, a content-based link building campaign can be extremely successful. This approach prioritizes creating a valuable asset that can be used to generate links. The type of content can vary depending on niche, so an infographic may be great for certain websites, whereas an in-depth white paper may be more appropriate for others. Whether you are striving for funny, relevant, or informative, the point is that having a high-quality link serves as a key differentiator for brands. When all else is equal, the volume and quality of links that point to a given page will help it shoot up the rankings.

Similarly, having exemplary content is the most important facet of SEO today since it greatly increases the odds of obtaining natural links from relevant pages across the internet. Put another way, the best websites only link to the very best websites. Creating quality content increases the odds of being linked by the most authoritative websites and blogs, thereby boosting your traffic and search results as well.

# WHY SEO MATTERS FROM A BUSINESS AND DIGITAL MARKETING PERSPECTIVE

At the outset of this chapter, I mentioned that adaptability is essential for success in the world of SEO. Well, it also just so happens that adaptability is essential for businesses. In other words, businesses that fail to adapt and react to the ever-changing world of SEO will get left behind by competitors who do adjust to the updates/changes. When SEO first arrived onto the scene in the 1990s, keyword stuffing, manual submission, and the meta keywords tags and the like were regular and standard practices for the industry. By the mid-2000s, link bombing with anchor text, buying links from automated spam injectors, and constructing interlinking farms of websites were widely used strategies. Now, imagine if a brand in 2016 and beyond tried to incorporate these strategies. Instead of helping their SEO efforts, they would be actively harming them as well as sabotaging the brand's reputation because Google's algorithm has grown extensively and now penalizes bad SEO practices.

Google's algorithm is actually a great look into just how quickly a field of digital marketing can change. What was sound SEO procedure a few years ago now looks outdated in retrospect, thanks to the constant algorithm changes that take place each year. For those interested in Google's algorithm changes, simply do a Google search for "Moz Google Algorithm Change History." Moz has put together an excellent snapshot of how Google algorithms have changed over the years.

Constant change, then, is the one constant of SEO and digital marketing. While constant change is a recurring theme of digital marketing as a whole, it is especially true for SEO. The history and evolution of SEO alone is testament to this fact, but these changes are not to say SEO is "dead," as some erroneously claim. Far from it, in fact. In 2012, research showed that the demand for SEO professionals was soaring, and in 2015, the demand for SEO positions continued to grow. Not only were SEO jobs up 18% in 2015, but the average salary continued to increase as well. These growth factors have propelled SEO into a $65 billion industry, leading some experts to question whether the industry will ever stop growing.

While staying ahead of competitors is one of the main reasons SEO matters to a business and/or brand, it is far from the only reason. Another critically important component of SEO's continued importance is the fact that SEO's market share continues growing. Eighty to ninety percent of customers check product reviews before making a purchase online, and finding product reviews means paying a visit to your preferred search engine. Even better, overhauling SEO is a cost-effective effort that can be used as a foundation of your online presence. Combine these factors, and it is clear that without an effort to implement cost-effective (and just plain effective) SEO, your potential customers will find competitors instead of your brand.

Despite the importance of SEO, it is important not overstate the significance of SEO as well. This is not meant to serve as a cryptic riddle, but rather as a reminder of the unified foundation of digital marketing as a whole. Brands and businesses looking to incorporate SEO should follow suit. SEO should never be implemented in a vacuum. In other words, email marketing, social media marketing, and other digital marketing strategies provide benefits that SEO cannot provide. That said, SEO also provides essential marketing advantages that other forms of digital marketing are not equipped to offer. SEO is a key element of a strong bedrock foundation for a brand's digital marketing efforts, but it should not be treated as the "end all and be all." However, it must not be dismissed, either.

The following case study is evidence on how SEO can be leveraged into a transformative marketing effort by combining various facets of digital marketing into the overall SEO effort.

## HOW IGN USED SEO TO TRANSFORM ITS WEBSITE INTO AN INTERNATIONALLY KNOWN BRAND

For anyone who loves video games, IGN should be a very familiar name. The gaming and pop culture-themed website is ranked as the 440th most popular website in the world, and it is now a premier destination for all things game related. While IGN is certainly enjoying success in 2016, things were not always so rosy.

In the summer of 2003, IGN was not the internationally renowned website it is today, but its SEO efforts put it on the path toward its success that it has achieved today. In 2003, IGN teamed with an SEO company since IGN's goals were to break into the search engine world and generate increased traffic from Google. With the SEO experts navigating the strategy, the brand achieved just that and then some.

The SEO company quickly determined that IGN's game reviews were not laid out in a manner that was in compliance with search engine ranking guidelines. The SEO company quickly fixed this issue, and the enhanced search results were nearly instantaneous. This relatively simple fix increased IGN's organic search traffic by a staggering 1,500%, which led to increased revenues as well.

This incredible influx of traffic led to the website's acquisition by News Corp for the princely sum of $650 million. Without SEO, IGN as an internationally recognized website would likely not exist, indicating just how important SEO can be when brands rely on SEO expertise to enhance their brand's organic traffic results.

## SKILLS NEEDED FOR A CAREER IN SEO

A career in SEO is one where intense competition is the normal state of events. Consider how many businesses there are fighting to get to the top page of Google rankings for any given keyword across thousands of industries and niches. The SEO digital marketing professional relishes this level of competition, seeing it as a unique opportunity to help brands have their voices heard in an increasingly crowded online space. Tenacity and the ability to view competition as an opportunity, then, is an absolute must. Still, one should have needs more than sheer tenacity to excel in SEO. Here are a few of the most important skills to master.

## GENUINE COMMITMENT TO THE BRANDS YOU TRANSFORM

Of course, the SEO marketer must also be committed to the brands they help. Nothing in life is permanent, and that is especially true in SEO. Even once a company gets to the top of search rankings, merely resting on that success practically guarantees they will not stay at the top for long. As such, an SEO marketer will continue to offer solutions that help brands stay at the top for the long haul, not just the short-term.

## BLEND CREATIVITY AND A LOVE FOR DATA TO STAND OUT IN SEO

SEO is also a great career path for both creative and analytics-driven individuals alike. For the analytics-driven person, technical SEO is going to offer plenty of opportunities to leverage data and analysis into meaningful, actionable brand opportunities. While the term may sound intimidating, technical SEO is really just a fancy way of describing the fact that a website needs a strong foundation for quality content the best chance to rank highly for relevant keywords and phrases. Like a house, then, SEO efforts are only as good as the foundation, and technical SEO professionals operate like an SEO architect.

Technical SEO will help make sure the site loads quickly, first and foremost, since slow websites harm SEO rankings. That said, an SEO professional does not simply guess what is wrong with the website's speed. Rather, this person uses analytics and data to determine the cause of a website's slowdown, fixing it at the foundational level. Technical SEO also involves testing the user-friendliness of all sites, especially mobile websites. Effectively, then, these professionals will do the analytics legwork needed to make sure all of a brand's website architecture is sound and working as intended. These efforts then let the creative individuals excel in a different area of SEO, which is the more well-known SEO practices of content creation and link building.

Make no mistake, technical SEO and creative SEO are equally important. One without the other is doomed to fail. Whether you are creative or analytics-driven, there is a place for you in SEO.

The following case study of a local Pennsylvania home contractor clearly shows the need for both technical and creative SEO marketing efforts. The home contractor in question had a tremendous offline reputation since the business was greatly valued by previous customers. Even so, this reputation did not translate online. They just were not making the splash they should be making based on their offline success.

This lack of SEO results caused them to reach out to an SEO firm who was tasked with helping them increase their share of the local residential market. To achieve this goal, the first thing the firm did was conduct a sophisticated and in-depth technical SEO audit aimed at using analytics to determine where the contractor's online presence could improve. Right away, the firm recognized numerous improvements that could be made to meet the latest technical SEO standards.

These technical improvements were paired with an online public relations campaign that leveraged creative aspects of SEO, which was designed to spread the word about the contractor's success and value proposition. This was achieved through links built to the website and a significant amount of quality content in relevant local publications and the home contractor's company blog.

With this two-fold SEO approach, of both technical and creative SEO, the contractor's organic traffic increased by 25% compared to the previous year. Even better, search engine traffic more than doubled, and the client ended up ranking for 393 keywords in the local area instead of just 18 keywords before contacting the SEO firm.

This case study demonstratively proves there is a place for you no matter where you fall on the creative vs. technical spectrum.

## SEO SPECIALIST

**Required Skills**
- A Working Knowledge of Search Engine Optimization Tools and Techniques
- The Ability to be Creative and Strategic while Identifying SEO Problems and Creating the Solutions
- A Familiarity with Google Analytics and Website Optimization Tools
- The Ability to Prepare Detailed Strategy Reports and Help Identify Valuable Keywords to Drive Traffic
- Keep an Eye on the Competition's SEO Efforts

**Expected Salary: $35,000 to $45,000**

A SEO specialist is expected to be familiar with managing and operating a brand's online traffic acquisition efforts. This begins with a working knowledge of search engine optimization tools and techniques that are necessary to succeed in this field. Google Analytics and website optimization tools are core tools that a specialist must be familiar with to create proven SEO strategies that are based on data that can lead to the development of effective link building and keyword techniques.

The specialist should also be equipped with the skills needed to both create detailed strategy reports and identify valuable keywords that will help drive the most valuable traffic toward the brand. Also of note is the specialist's responsibility of analyzing client websites for areas that can be improved and optimized to benefit SEO rankings.

Additionally, the specialist should monitor the efforts of competitors, noting the techniques and keywords that are being used. Keeping an eye on the competition could help the specialist see what is and is not working for other SEO professionals, which can be leveraged into creating better SEO strategies.

## SEO ANALYST

### Required Skills

* Experience with Keyword Research and SEO Optimization
* Ideation Strategies for New Content That Will Improve Search Rankings
* Working with Content Teams to Provide SEO Analysis, Advice and Best Practices
* Keep Tabs on the Competition, Reverse Engineering Successful SEO Strategies
* Ability to Work With SEO Tools to Provide Detailed Reports and Analysis

### Expected Salary: $40,000 to $55,000

SEO analyst assesses and analyzes a brand or agency's SEO efforts. Once the SEO strategies and implementations are analyzed, the analyst must then optimize SEO efforts, which likely includes formulating content ideas that drive qualified traffic to a website. Ideal candidates who land preferred SEO analyst positions should have experience with keyword research, SEO optimization, and providing SEO guidance and actionable insights.

Beyond these requirements, it is preferable for a hopeful analyst to possess analytics and reporting skills for analysis of website content. With these skills, an SEO analyst is able to keep close tabs on industry competitors, taking note of their SEO tactics and strategies. This is important for two reasons. First, an analyst can pick up on tactical errors competitors are making, helping the analyst's brand from making the same tactical mishaps. Second, and more importantly, an analyst can discern the competitor's successful strategies and SEO innovations, helping the analyst's company reverse engineer them to enjoy similar successes.

To achieve these goals, familiarity with SEO tools such as keyword tools, Google Search Console, Moz, Searchmetrics, and/or SEMrush should prove fruitful. For reference, Google Search Console—formerly Google Webmasters Tool—is a free SEO tool that helps analysts track indexing and crawling statistics while also using metrics that aid in optimizing websites for higher visibility. Valuable tools like these help an SEO analyst have the technical expertise needed to implement SEO strategies for sustained success.

## SEO MANAGER

**Required Skills**
- The Ability to Optimize Websites and Boost Search Rankings Both for Clients and Internally
- Perform Extensive Audits that Help the SEO Department Develop Comprehensive Keyword Strategies
- An Understanding of Both Technical and Creative SEO
- Effective Use of SEO Tools to Increase Rankings, Effectively Increasing Leads, and Sales Via Organic Search
- Mastery of Fundamentals Like Google Webmaster Tools, Meta Tags, Link Anchor Text, and Page Titles

**Expected Salary: $65,000 to $95,000**

The SEO Manager is a key employee in an organization's digital marketing efforts, and it is who most specialists directly report to within the department. Depending on the size and scope of the company, an SEO manager may be in charge of a single account or may instead take on many accounts for the company. This type of work typically occurs at companies who provide SEO services for clients, helping them optimize websites and boost their search rankings, as shown in this chapter's case studies.

Alternatively, some companies may be looking to hire an SEO manager to shore up their own internal SEO issues. Either way, the function of an SEO manager is likely the same.

The manager can be expected to develop comprehensive keyword strategies for better rankings after performing extensive SEO audits. Using SEO tools like Moz or BrightEdge, the findings of SEO keyword research, backlink profile analysis and technical SEO review give managers the insight needed to increase rankings, which thereby increases leads and sales through organic search.

Demonstrable skill with Google Webmaster tools (Google Tag manager, Google Analytics) is expected, as is mastery of key SEO fundamentals like meta tags, headers, URL structure, link anchor text, and page titles.

## DIRECTOR OF SEO

**Required Skills**

- Prioritizing Organic Search Engine Results by Developing a Strong Understanding of the Client's Competition, Industry, Marketing Goals, and Objectives
- Ability to Foster Teamwork at All Levels of the Organization
- Ability to Think Strategically and Pass on the Strategic Vision to Teams Working Under the SEO Director
- Develop and Execute High End Strategies
- Continue to Innovate and Drive Organic Search Results

**Expected Salary: $90,000 to $110,000**

SEO professionals spend their time focusing on page listings that a marketer cannot pay for, and the SEO Director works to ensure these professionals excel in all aspects of SEO. The director heads the entire SEO department, developing the strategies that must be executed by SEO managers and their employees.

Because SEO professionals prioritize non-paid search results, an SEO director's job duties will prioritize continuous innovation in ways that enhance organic search rankings. To do so, an SEO director needs to develop a strong understanding of the company's competition, as well as the company's own marketing goals and objectives within the respective industry.

With this understanding comes the director's ability to effectively manage and oversee the company's collaboration to ensure the SEO vision is fulfilled. To that end, the director must be a proven team leader who is capable of keeping the ship on course at all times.

If this job title is something you aspire to reach one day, know that building quality links is increasingly important in the world of SEO. As such, any SEO job hopefuls should start gaining familiarity with link building now. Taking courses or experimenting with building quality links firsthand will give you the familiarity needed to showcase your experience in this area. There are plenty of free and affordable educational resources that can teach you how to build high-quality links that drive relevant traffic to websites.

## VP OF GROWTH MARKETING

**Required Skills**
- Lead All Digital Marketing Departments by Pursuing Growth Strategies for Every Department
- The Ability to Cross-Collaborate With All Departments, Clearly Explaining the Larger Digital Marketing Vision
- Can Conceptualize and Implement Inbound Marketing Strategies to Achieve Market Targets for All Departments
- Develop and Execute High-end Strategies
- Oversee the Daily Activities of Each Department, Making Sure the Departments Are on Track to Meet Specified Goals

**Expected Salary: $130,000+**

The final rung in the career progression of the SEO career professional is often VP of Growth Marketing. Once a professional shows he or she is an SEO master capable of growing SEO results to new heights, the next evolution is to grow the results of the entire marketing team.

As a result, the VP of Growth Marketing will be tasked with growing just about every department related to digital marketing. SEO, SEM, digital analytics, social media, eCommerce, and all other marketing departments need growth, and the VP is tasked purely with strategizing how to make this happen in each marketing department.

Fortunately, a career in SEO cross-collaborates with many other marketing departments as we have discussed. For this reason, success in SEO prepares a professional for this role as well as one could hope.

A VP should be able to conceptualize and implement inbound marketing strategies to achieve market targets for each department. To do this, the VP must be adept and skilled at market research and planning. Using the analytics skills one has learned over the course of a career will prove instrumental in this endeavor, as it gives the VP the data needed to implement effective growth strategies.

Once strategies are in place, the VP must oversee each department's day-to-day marketing activities to ensure each team's execution of the strategy is meeting outlined goals. If a VP's plan successfully comes together, the brand and its digital marketing efforts will soar to new heights.

## GETTING STARTED ON THE PATH TOWARD AN SEO CAREER

Before you can hang your hat on being an SEO master, get started by grasping the basics. In SEO (and digital marketing, generally), it is best to learn by doing. Plenty of online and classroom training resources are available to take your SEO skills to the next level, and many of them are free. To that end, the SEO Training Course by Moz is a free and informative way to take your first foray into understanding SEO in a meaningful way. Moz's guide has been read more than 3 million times and continues to be one of the better freely available resources for SEO understanding.

After you have learned the basics from your chosen SEO educational resources, there are a number of advanced steps you can take that will help you out on your path toward SEO mastery. For one, start a blog. You may be questioning the merits of including a blog as an advanced SEO step. Well, it certainly is not an advanced step toward SEO mastery if you treat the blog like the average blogger does. Treat it as an experiment in SEO deserving of your full attention. It is certainly an advanced education on what makes for effective SEO.

With a blog, you are basically learning firsthand what has and has not worked for your blog's search ranking efforts. For the analytical (a skill that is greatly valued in SEO), starting a blog offers critical insight into the data-driven facets of SEO. Often, words are the great draw to the world of SEO, and for good reason. It is words that are used in Google searches (more often than not, at least), so it is words that drive Google results. Regardless, it is numbers and raw data that helps SEO professionals analyze precisely how words and search terms achieve success or failure in search results.

Additionally, blogging will provide valuable lessons about the importance of fresh content. Try implementing all the best backlinking, keyword, and social media strategies without fresh content that is valuable and informative. You will quickly find that results will be mixed at best. In this way, a blog is a great tool to teach how various areas of digital marketing intersect and coincide. The best blogs excel at leveraging written content, images, video, keyword optimization, backlinks, social media (and its influencers), and more to great effect. As such, if you have not yet mastered keyword optimization or certain other areas of SEO essential best practices, treat a blog as a valuable teaching tool.

In this way, starting a career in SEO is a great way to launch into other digital marketing careers. SEO is a great career choice in itself, but it may not be a career you wish to pursue exclusively. This does not matter because SEO is one of the most important skills one can attain in all of digital marketing. Even if, years later, it is only one facet of your entire digital marketing skillset, it will still reap dividends. SEO expert Ross Hudgens says SEO can be thought of as a large set of skills, like being good with people or an exemplary writer. While these are exceedingly valuable skills, other skills must accompany them in order to maximize their value.

Today, SEO is commonly integrated into other marketing departments and processes, ensuring that you will not be confined to SEO if you look to branch out later in a career. SEO rarely acts as a standalone department. Instead, it tends to be incorporated into other digital marketing departments for maximum success, such as the social media department. The reason for this is SEO plays a crucial role in unifying the entire marketing effort's message. As such, if you are an adaptable individual who embraces the ideas of a potential career change and remaining flexible, SEO could have your name on it. Adaptability and flexibility are not the only tools you will need to thrive as an SEO professional, however.

Enthusiasm is also of the utmost importance. Designing compelling link building strategies and strategizing on the ways a brand can maximize search rankings through quality content creation is a thrill like few others, but actually doing the work can be a grind, like any other job. By enthusiasm, then, what I mean is remaining enthusiastic about making a difference for all your clients. Whether you help a small business grow exponentially or help a large corporation continue to stay ahead of its competitors, you're making a difference.

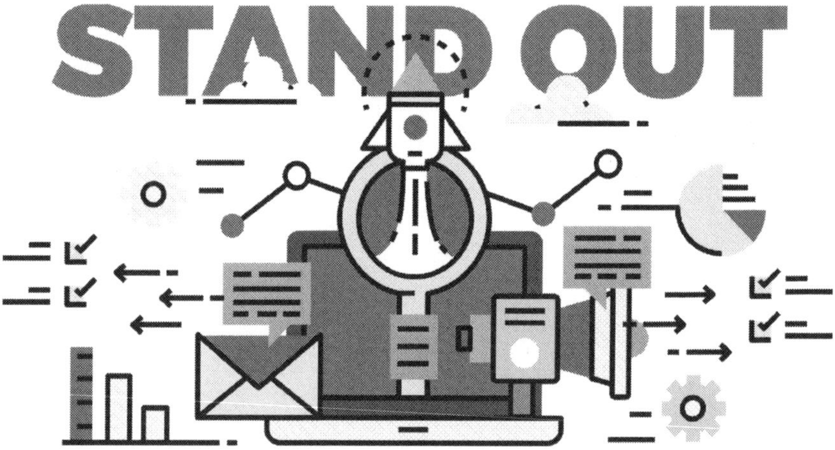
STAND OUT

# 10

GETTING NOTICED IN
A CROWDED DIGITAL
MARKETING FIELD

## WHAT YOU WILL LEARN IN THIS CHAPTER:

* How to Write a Resume that Commands Attention
* Unlocking the Secrets of What Hiring Managers Look for in a Digital Marketer
* How to Win the Job Interview Before It Begins
* The Characteristics of the Successful Digital Marketer
* What Does Establishing a Successful Digital Marketing Career Hinge Upon?

Much of the discussion in previous chapters has centered around the jobs you can find in the diverse areas of digital marketing. While each of these previous chapters offer advice on gaining the specific experience needed for a respective digital marketing field, there is a great degree of overlap in digital marketing. Due to this overlap, there are broad principles you can use to stand out in digital marketing, no matter what field you wish to pursue.

This chapter is dedicated to exploring these broader themes that will prove fruitful in a job search.

This chapter is for the dedicated job searchers who, for whatever reason, simply have not landed a job in their preferred field of digital marketing. The most diligent job searchers start by covering the basics. You have an absolutely impeccable and error-free resume. You took the online coursework you needed and finely honed your digital marketing skills. Perhaps you even went the extra mile and sent thank you notes to your respective interviewers when you were job hunting. If all those efforts have not landed you the dream job you are seeking, do not lose hope. By 2020, an additional 150,000 digital marketing jobs are expected. In short, there is room for you in this field. It is just a matter of standing out in a positive and forward thinking manner.

Meeting the criteria is one thing, but mastering the job interview is another entirely. This chapter will equip you with the skills needed to stand out, but know that the key to standing out in your interview (and digital marketing in general) boils down to preparation. According to Jane Creaner-Glen, head of recruitment and HR at the Digital Marketing Institute, a "great digital marketing interview is all in the preparation. By the time you walk through the door it is too late to do anything. Make sure you check out the LinkedIn profiles of the people you are meeting and also look on LinkedIn for people in the company within the team you will be joining...That will give you an idea of the ideal background for the role and also the level you will be expected to work at."

In addition to this excellent advice, also make sure to learn about the company itself. Learn about more than just the company's strengths. It is arguably more important to discern some of the company's weaknesses that you can help the company improve. After all, you are a potential hire because the company needs skills or qualities you can provide. Show an employer you are the person to provide these solutions and can independently do the homework ahead of time.

Preparing in this way will provide key insights into the company culture, helping you assess the personal fit for the role. Being able to actually do the job is important, but arguably, these personal characteristics are even more important. Plenty of job applicants will have the skills and educational background to succeed, but fewer will be a good fit for the employer's company culture. This is where you can stand out.

## WRITING A RESUME THAT GRABS A HIRING MANAGER'S ATTENTION

In the world of digital marketing, knowing your target audience is a core component of establishing yourself as an expert in your field. Marketing campaigns hinge on knowing who to reach and how to speak their language. Why? Once you know who your target audience is, other decisions and strategies become easier.

Similarly, your resume needs to be written with your target audience in mind. In a word, you are writing for the typical hiring manager in digital marketing. If you know what the typical hiring manager hopes to read and find in your resume, you can tailor a precisely crafted message that resonates. However, to do this, you must understand the type of job and company to which you are applying.

There are a few questions to ask yourself when crafting your resume. For example, find out whether the job is exclusively digital marketing in nature, or whether it will combine traditional marketing and digital work. Further, what is the company's makeup? Are you applying to an ad agency with established digital teams and vast resources, or are you applying to a small company looking to make the most out of a modest digital marketing budget? Asking questions of this nature will help you create an initial outline of what is important to the company and the job role you seek. By extension, you will know what the hiring manager is looking for in your resume.

Additionally, following the advice of Jane Creaner-Glen mentioned earlier, take the time to find out more about the company culture as well. Creaner-Glen recommended LinkedIn, but also consider taking the time to browse a company's Instagram. Taking a look at these photos will give you a "behind the scenes" look into the workplace setting and the fun side of the company. You can use your findings as inspiration for your resume, while learning valuable insights into the companies you are hoping to work for after a successful interview and hiring process.

Armed with this knowledge, highlight the skills and traits in your background and experience that are most reflective of what the hiring manager needs in an employee. In many fields of digital marketing, keywords are important, and so it goes with your resume as well. Carefully select keywords and aspects of your background that will leap off the page for your target audience. Similarly, know which keywords should not be used. In general, it is better to show, not tell. Avoid using terms like "go-getter" or "team player."

These generic phrases have been shown to harm a prospective job seeker. Instead of "go-getter," show an employer how your drive and initiative pushed you to succeed in school or at an internship. Similarly, show how you manage and/or work well with others instead of relying on the impersonal "team player" phrase. Other keywords to avoid include calling yourself "dynamic," "creative," and "passionate." If these traits are true, these qualities should be effortlessly conveyed with a quality resume, rather than relying on forced and overused slogans.

The great irony of crafting a targeted message is that you are applying for a digital marketing job while marketing yourself. Thus, you are already signaling to a potential marketer what kind of digital marketer you will be. Merely knowing what the hiring manager wants to read is only the first step of creating a standout resume.

The second step, once again, echoes a recurring principle of digital marketing writ large. Namely, you need to define what makes you unique. There are a unique sets of characteristics, experiences, skillsets, and life stories that make you who and what you are. Leaving this narrative off the pages of your resume is a mistake too many hopeful job applicants make. Why wait until you are in the middle of an interview to begin telling your story? Your resume provides an excellent opportunity to convey what makes you authentic and the ideal fit for the job. You need to show a hiring manager why you are valuable.

A great example of this comes by way of Nina4Airbnb, a website started by a woman who wanted to gain employment with the Airbnb company. Nina Mufleh, the website creator, took a brilliantly proactive approach by showing Airbnb precisely why she was valuable. Namely, she took it upon herself to show Airbnb why, despite their international success, their success rates in the Middle East were far lower than they should be. Nina's website created a clear roadmap paving a path for Airbnb to enhance their results in the Middle East, which included tapping into the lucrative potential of the Dubai market. Before long, the CEO of Airbnb noticed Nina's unconventional resume, which gained her valuable attention that helped advance her career. The key takeaway of Nina's story is that the resume is more than just a list of accomplishments and qualifications. Rather, it is the perfect opportunity to show why you are an ideal fit for a company's vision in an authentic and compelling why. Do that, and just like Nina's, your resume may end up going viral and being shared by the Huffington Post.

Practically speaking, you need to demonstrate why you are a cut above the rest of the job applicants. Think about the unique skills and knowledge you have accrued, as well as how you can best convey these unique traits in a meaningful way. For example, if you are applying for a social media digital marketing position, highlighting your talent for creating viral videos to drive sales growth will garner positive attention. Again, the value proposition you convey about yourself will hinge on the type of job and company you target. Large agencies will look for completely different skills compared to a small business or a large corporation. Just as you are unique, so too are the jobs and companies you are applying to for employment. Therefore, think about what makes you unique, and then apply those traits to the unique job and company culture.

Finally, like all things marketing, your resume needs a winning strategy. Writing a targeted, unique resume is quite difficult, if not outright impossible, without a strategic plan of action. Before digital marketing results are ever attained, a quality plan is developed. Similarly, your resume strategy will go a long way toward getting you the job you need.

A great example of putting these principles into action comes by way of 21-year-old Sumukh Mehta, who managed to be hired by GQ, an internationally recognized men's magazine, simply by creating a standout resume. Specifically, Sumukh created a resume that looked like it was lifted directly from the pages of GQ itself, designed to look like a GQ issue complete with a professional cover and a professional model shoot. Naturally, when GQ recognized that their job applicant was capable of creating the look and feel of the magazine itself, they knew this was an applicant that needed to become

an employee in short order. GQ was so enamored with the resume and Sumukh's standout approach that he was hired without needing an interview.

Using the examples of Nina and Sumukh, ask yourself how you can take a
similarly unique approach to land that dream job. Here are a few questions
to ask yourself when devising a resume strategy:

  * What skills are employers hoping to see in the resume?
  * What is the best layout and structural design for your resume to exceed the
    hiring manager's expectations?
  * How can you highlight what makes you unique?
  * If possible, can you give real world examples of what makes you valuable
    (campaigns you have successfully run, ideas you created that were a success,
    proven results, etc.)?

To summarize, your resume must:

  * Be Written with the Target Audience (Hiring Manager) in Mind
  * Convey What Makes You Uniquely Valuable
  * Have a Consistent Messaging Strategy That Makes the Target Audience
    Instinctively Understand Why You Are an Ideal Fit for the Job

Meet these benchmarks, and you are well on your way toward earning a
chance to interview for the job. Before you ever step foot in the interview
room, know what hiring managers look for at a digital marketing job interview.

## WHAT HIRING MANAGERS LOOK FOR IN JOB APPLICANTS

Digital marketing jobs abound. The U.S. Bureau of Labor Statistics forecasts
that employment will rise 7% by 2024 for digital marketing. Given the importance of digital marketing to a company's revenue and bottom line, it is
a great field for long-term stability. Still, hiring managers struggle to find
talent. Plenty of digital marketing hiring managers should have U2's "I Still
Haven't Found what I'm Looking for" as the permanent soundtrack of their
hiring process. In other words, there is a gap in digital marketing skills due
to the high rate of change in the industry. What, then, is the first thing you
can do to stand out with a hiring manager? For starters, you can show that

you are adaptable and embrace change, gaining digital marketing skills as soon as they are needed. There is a reason that embracing change and remaining adaptable have been recurring themes throughout this book. It is the surest way to get a job in this field.

However, it is essential to clarify what I mean by having the right digital marketing skills. Just about every applicant will have the bare minimum "required skills" for a job. That is fine, but it is not what a hiring manager "hopes" to see. The bare minimum is what a hiring manager expects to see. Rather, it is an applicant's ability to go beyond the bare minimum of attaining specific digital marketing skills that helps the applicant "wow" a hiring manager. Too many applicants have plenty of experience in their field, while being sorely lacking in other aspects of digital marketing. Today's digital marketing has such a great degree of crossover that most employers want an applicant to have at least surface-level knowledge of other fields of digital marketing.

In simplified terms, be a T-shaped digital marketer. This term refers to the fact that digital marketers of the future must have deep knowledge and ability in one field of digital marketing while also having basic knowledge and functionality in many other digital marketing disciplines. The end result is that the digital marketer will be capable of handling the vast majority of issues that arise on the job.

Effectively, hiring managers hope to see that you are a lifelong student of digital marketing. The reason is that marketing will continue to undergo rapid transformations in the near future. Naturally, this will also change the priorities of a hiring manager, but guess what will not change? The lifelong learners who adapt to the change and continue learning the latest skills and digital marketing developments will always be highly sought after in the job market.

Additionally, this is not to say you should not have specialized skills as a digital marketer. In previous chapters, recall that plenty of job titles we discussed came with the title of "Specialist." Specialized expertise is a positive, but it should never come at the expense of seeing how all of digital marketing is unified. We have talked previously about the unifying foundation of digital marketing in the book's introduction, which stresses that varying areas of digital marketing work together in unison.

Put another way, do not become overly reliant on your specialty. The field of digital marketing moves quickly, so mastering one area of digital marketing alone could leave your expertise outdated, instead of "job secure." You need to be able to see how your specialized expertise can gel with other areas of a company's digital marketing efforts, allowing you to branch out and add more skills to your digital marketing "toolset." Put another way, technology is constantly changing, so you are going to need to remain an adaptable and eager learner who constantly helps the team succeed.

What follows is a list of desirable qualities that almost any digital marketing employer will view as a plus when it comes to making a hire. When reading the following sections, take an honest assessment of your interview skills and find ways to perfect your strengths and refine any areas that can be improved. In so doing, rest assured you will separate yourself from fellow job seekers while strengthening your odds of landing your ideal digital marketing job.

## CHARACTERISTICS OF THE SUCCESSFUL DIGITAL MARKETER

### Effective Communication

While technical expertise is certainly to be valued, it is equally important to focus on your personality and character traits when pursuing a job. In digital marketing, interpersonal communication skills are exceedingly important in almost every facet of the industry. Being able to communicate effectively across departments will help build strong relationships and a better company culture, which is obviously helpful. However, even social media marketing campaigns, email newsletters, and the like depend on a marketer's ability to deftly understand how to communicate with a target audience.

### Relationship Building

Marketing is about relationship building, first and foremost, so your ability to build those relationships will speak volumes during the hiring process. The ideal digital marketer should be able to work effectively with all internal teams with fruitful collaboration. Even if you land a job in this field, do not expect to last long if you cannot work well with others and collaborate in the pursuit of team-oriented success.

## Adaptability

The ideal digital marketer must also adapt. This book has covered adaptability a great deal, but primarily in the context of adapting to the changing world of digital marketing. Adaptability is just as important from a company standpoint. Since digital marketing is constantly changing, so too are corporations, small businesses, and digital marketing agencies. With this change comes an organization's need to test out new ideas and features on websites and across their marketing efforts.

However, these responses to change will only be as successful if the employees are adaptable and prepared to change course and try new solutions at any moment. Even within the context of a single marketing campaign, if research and analysis highlights the need for a new strategy, digital marketers must be prepared to execute the new strategy rapidly. As such, the changing nature of marketing makes inter-office adaptability one of the most important skills a digital marketer can possess.

## See the Big Picture

A natural extension of the need for interpersonal skills and adaptability, employers expect their digital marketers to see the big picture of company goals. In two words, digital marketers need to have good "business sense." Good business sense is not limited to senior executives and C-level decision makers, either. While it is certainly an essential for business leaders, companies today need all digital marketers to have a grasp on the pulse of a business's daily responsibilities and departmental goals.

Why? Businesses are quickly realizing the landscape of marketing has shifted. Consumers today want authentic and transparent marketing that has a finger on the pulse of what society and consumers want. The best digital marketers will have an intuitive understanding of these desires and will be able to convey these needs to C-suite decision makers. In this way, digital marketers help businesses connect the dots from an abstract marketing goal into a tangibly meaningful marketing implementation.

If digital marketing job applicants have the business acumen that helps them see how their daily job functions relate to departmental strategy and overall company success, the "applicants" will quickly become fixtures within the company's digital marketing teams.

To recap, there are four key characteristics you can sharpen to stand out to recruiters and/or hiring managers. Those characteristics are the following:

1. Effective Interpersonal Communication Skills to Foster Strong Relationships and a Better Company Culture
2. The Desire to Build Strong Relationships that Promote a Better Workplace Environment for the Team
3. The Ability to Adapt to Changes in the Workplace as Digital Marketing Evolves
4. Seeing the Big Picture of How Individual Efforts Help a Company Realize and Execute Marketing Goals

With these skills in hand, combined with proper digital marketing experience, you are well on your way to winning the interview and landing your preferred digital marketing position. There are, however, additional steps you can take to "win" the interview before it even begins.

## WINNING THE INTERVIEW BEFORE IT EVEN BEGINS

Assuming you have an ideal resume and the experience needed to make you an attractive hire, you still have to nail the interview. For this reason, plenty of people find the interview process to be a nervous and daunting experience. The best way to alleviate a case of nerves before an interview is by exhaustively researching and preparing for the interview. Not only will this give you confidence, it will also signal to the interviewer that you take the job opportunity seriously. These benefits make it imperative that you do your research before the interview.

To keep matters simple, here are five key areas to research prior to having a digital marketing job interview:

1. Research How Your Experience and Background Fits Within the Job's Requirements
2. Find Out What Objectives the Brand Is Trying to Achieve

3. Explore What the Brand Is Already Doing with Their Online Presence
4. Look into Various Marketing Channels Such as SEO, Social Media, and Company Newsletters
5. Use What You Have Learned To Pour into a Highly Focused and Personalized Resume and Cover Letter

Jot down some notes as you research because your findings will be instrumental to navigating the interview. Make sure your notes are brief, easily memorized, and on message. With these notes, you will be able to personalize your experiences and demonstrate how your unique values can help the brand improve its digital marketing strategy and results. In plenty of interviews, you will be asked for suggestions or feedback regarding the company's marketing and culture. These questions exist for a reason, and having a nuanced answer is your perfect chance to conclusively demonstrate you are the right person for the job. Once your resume lands you an interview, do not assume your work is finished until interview time. Research, research, and research some more. Many dream jobs have been landed by applicants who do their research and go the extra mile during the hiring process.

When it comes to doing this essential research, do yourself a favor and take the two minutes needed to watch Ramit Sethi's briefcase technique. Sethi's intuition when developing the proven briefcase technique is that 80% of the work in an interview or salary negotiation happens before the meeting ever takes place.

The general upshot of the briefcase technique is that you pull ideas out of your hypothetical briefcase citing ways a business can improve and the steps needed to do it. Thousands of job applicants have landed their ideal job by following this simple and timeless advice. Ramit provides a helpful case study of the briefcase technique in action with a testimonial from Beth G., a grateful recipient of the approach who landed her dream job.

Beth found her dream job browsing idealist.org, and decided to write a focused cover letter keeping the principles of the briefcase technique in mind. The end result was a tailored resume, showing her dream company the key areas she could dominate for the company to improve their results. Then, she networked her way into a job interview by leveraging her connections. Beth's boss and mentor knew important people at the company she hoped to work for, which helped her land the interview. That said, Beth did not wait and simply hope that her connections alone were enough to land the job. Instead, she got busy crafting a project proposal for the last grant the company had received. Once the interview reached the midway point, Beth pulled the proposal out of her briefcase and began explaining in detail how the proposal could be implemented for the company immediately.

Beth quickly landed the job with a master's degree, while she was competing with three Ph.D.-level applicants. In this way, Beth won the battle before ever stepping into the interview room. Do your research by implementing the briefcase technique, and similar successes should come naturally.

## MAKING THE INTERVIEW AN UNMITIGATED SUCCESS

If you have followed this chapter's roadmap to success, you are already prepared for everything a job interview can throw your way. Knowledge, as they say, is power. You now have the confidence to enter any interview room and know you are ready to tell your story. View this as the incredible opportunity it is! After all the hours, months and—in some cases—years of study and preparation in digital marketing, you get the chance to convey what you have learned in a manner that showcases your unique talents. This, in a nutshell, is your championship game. All the information in this book has led to this moment, in much the same manner as years of preparation hone an MVP-caliber athlete for one final game to win the title.

Do not waste this opportunity by being a generic job applicant just trying to "say the right things." This is your moment to be uniquely you and let the chips fall where they may. Why would you not want to? It is your unique knowledge, background, and experience that have allowed you to accomplish so much. Trust the process one more time, let the authentic "you" shine through, and land the job you have worked so hard to pursue.

With that said, there is still an ideal way to tell your story in a compelling way. First and foremost, understand that a hiring manager or interviewer is not here for a social visit. They are a busy employee in a busy 21st century world. Make sure, then, that your stories are concise, prepared, and direct. In other words, master your elevator pitch.

Nothing ruins a great interview like a rambling story that has no end in sight. Take the time to prepare a few of your best and most decisive digital marketing stories that celebrate your unique persona and showcase your successes and achievements. If you have yet to attain digital marketing experience and are applying for an entry level role, leverage your previous work experience or education to show you are a passionate and dedicated employee who is serious about starting a career in marketing. Again, tell a story that weaves a compelling narrative of a young, bright individual with a strong work ethic who is excited about launching into a digital marketing career. These stories ought to be presented in a humble, coherent, and confident manner, and each story should highlight one theme above all else. Namely, that you are the candidate who is best suited to succeed in the role for which you are interviewing.

In this way, your elevator pitch should mimic the proven formula for a start-up company's pitch. Startups have long known that a concise, practiced description of your company vision should be riveting and empowering, but should also last only as long as it takes to ride up an elevator. Following this framework, your pitch should accomplish the following:

1. Introduce Yourself
2. Identify the Solutions You Will Provide for a Business's Problems
3. Offer Proof You Can Truly Deliver These Solutions
4. Plan for Next Steps after These Solutions Are Implemented

How can you tell your personal story in this direct and compelling way? Take a look at the resume you have spent time and energy perfecting. The roadmap will be found in that resume and the job description. Go through every requirement for the job point by point, making notes of similar successes you have achieved as a digital marketer. With this rough framework, then double back and expand on each point. You will likely find three to five great stories that can be drafted in a concise and powerfully effective manner. Additionally, get specific, using numbers wherever possible.

Take the interviewer on a journey where you had a key performance indicator (KPI) you needed to achieve in a certain timeframe. Walk them through the journey with you, showing them the steps you took and the hard-earned results you gave to an employer. Above all else, allowing a hiring manager to share in your personal journey will clearly demonstrate your passion for digital marketing. Let them know digital marketing is not "just another job" for you. It is something you wake up excited to do.

By following the advice laid out in this chapter, I have no doubt you will be empowered to stand out in a crowded job field and seize the opportunity that is right for you. Know, however, that landing your first job in digital marketing is merely the first step of the journey. If digital marketing is a lifelong passion for you, as it has been for me, getting hired is the first step of your career. Where you go from here is ultimately up to you, but know that for the passionate and creative innovator, digital marketing will always be a wonderful place to call home.

INTENTIONALLY LEFT BLANK

# HOW TO FIND THE PERFECT DIGITAL MARKETING CAREER

## WHAT YOU WILL LEARN IN THIS CHAPTER:

* Why Steve Jobs' Stanford Commencement Speech Should Inform Your Job Search
* Do the Hard Work to Land Your Dream Job
* A Key to the Job Search is Knowing How to Market Yourself to Get Your Dream Job
* Why Bold and Decisive Action Aids Your Job Search
* How Research Greatly Enhances Your Odds of Landing the Dream Job
* Once You Land the Dream Job, Plan for What's Next

For a digital marketing job hopeful looking to start their career, the good news is there are hundreds and thousands of digital marketing positions and opportunities out there, as evidenced by a search on LinkedIn or popular online job platforms. Conversely, some job hopefuls may find the job opportunities overwhelming, or they may not see the thousands of opportunities waiting to be seized after a quick search for "digital marketing jobs" in Google. With that said, plenty of job results will turn up, but these may not even be the best opportunities for you. Perhaps you will be overqualified for certain jobs or perhaps others will simply not interest you, which is why knowing where to look is half the battle when it comes to finding a great digital marketing career.

As Steve Jobs said during his acclaimed Stanford commencement speech to the Class of 2005, "Sometimes life hits you in the head with a brick. Don't lose faith. I'm convinced that the only thing that kept me going was that I loved what I did. You've got to find what you love. And that is as true for your work as it is for your lovers. Your work is going to fill a large part of your life, and the only way to be truly satisfied is to do what you believe is great work. And the only way to do great work is to love what you do. If you haven't found it yet, keep looking. Don't settle. As with all matters of the heart, you'll know it when you find it. And, like any great relationship, it just gets better and better as the years roll on. So keep looking until you find it. Don't settle."

While Jobs was speaking to an audience of graduates who went on to pursue a number of different careers in a wide range of industries, he might as well have been speaking exclusively to the digital marketing job hopeful. Still, it is important to keep Jobs' quote in its proper context. He is not saying "do not settle" until you find the perfect career. It will take time and effort to continue working in the industry until your dream job is found. What is meant, simply, is that you should never settle until you find a job you love.

Regardless of your interests, there are thousands of great jobs in digital marketing that will help you find a position you love. This chapter segments the available opportunities into easy to understand categories such as job boards, social media, and job aggregators, to name a few. Your job search should incorporate all of these tools into your job search, and the following sections will equip you with the knowledge needed to take advantage of these job search resources.

# JOB BOARDS/PORTALS

When it comes to the best employment websites, the usual suspects make an appearance here as well. We are talking about job search platforms like Monster, CareerBuilder, The Ladders, Dice, and even Craigslist. Another excellent resource to consider is MarketingHire, a website dedicated to all sorts of marketing jobs both traditional and digital. The general theme of these websites are one and the same, however, which is to find you a great digital marketing job.

These websites should be a part of your job search arsenal, to be sure, but do not forget about other digital marketing-focused employment websites such as the Direct Marketing Association. Similarly, there may be local associations that provide digital marketing opportunities in your area.

Given all these opportunities on employment websites alone, it will help to cull your use of employment websites to a select two or three best resources. This will not be stretching your job search net too thin since you will be using other job hunting resources to better diversify your approach to the job search.

Having said that, you are likely left wondering how to make the most out of the jobs posted on employment websites. It is a good question since merely filling out information and generically applying will not work. The digital marketing field receives too many job applications and resumes for such an approach to work. Instead, let us take a look at how one successful digital marketing job applicant utilized these resources to land a dream job.

In digital marketing, the joy is in the journey, and success may not come on the first day. In this next example, the applicant in question did not land him his initial dream job, but his positive attitude and passion for his dream job has led to becoming a successful entrepreneur and creator of a successful sports website. Just like Steve Jobs—who mentioned being fired from Apple as a setback that led to much of his later life success—overcoming obstacles is often an essential way to land the job of your dreams.

# HOW TO LAND A DREAM JOB

In this case, Rob Cressy asked his readers what steps they would take to land their dream job? For Rob, an avid sports fan, he came across a job posting on an employment website that would have him working for Bill Simmons. For those who are uninterested in sports, the simple takeaway is that Simmons is a prominent sports personality who has hosted shows on ESPN and created the highly celebrated sports website, Grantland.

In any case, Cressy saw this job posting, which was looking for someone who could create sports content and convey the right tone on social media. Cressy had spent more than three years doing just that at his own website, Bacon Sports, and he had followed Simmons for more than 15 years. As such, he felt confident in his ability to nail the tone and land the job as social media director. To stand out, Rob Cressy created a hilarious and targeted video message, talking about his accomplishments and creative ability in a way that would resonate with Bill Simmons. Part of this included wearing every jersey he owned, including an old-school Dana Barros jersey of Simmons' beloved hometown team, the Boston Celtics. Cressy's larger-than-life personality was on full-display in the video, which was great because the job application was authentically "him." Watch the over the top attempt at landing his dream job yourself, and you will see why he has gone on to entrepreneurial success in these fields. He clearly loves what he does.

With the video, he also crafted a tailored resume and sent the package to Bill Simmons' team. The total cost was $7, a couple hours of time and a lot of creativity. Did he land the job? No. But what he did do is showcase why he has become a successful entrepreneur via his sports website, Bacon Sports, and his digital marketing-focused website, Cress Media. While his dream job might not have been landed, it could very well be said that Cressy is already living the dream.

His first 1.5 years out of college, he was jobless and living off his credit card. Then, he found himself working dead-end, entry level jobs that were not taking him where he wanted to go. Eventually, Rob quit those jobs and got into digital marketing, becoming a full-time entrepreneur with Bacon Sports and Cress Media. This type of mentality is what will land you the job of your dreams. When you come across a listing on an employment website, imagine the job as more than just words on a computer screen. Imagine where it will take you and if it is a step in the journey toward loving what you do. If the answer is yes, then apply in a creative way that only you can. Not only will you increase your odds of getting the job by standing out in a creative way, you will also be refusing to settle for anything less than a job you love, as Steve Jobs suggested.

## COMPANY WEBSITES

Employment websites and job aggregators are a sort of middleman that connects job hopefuls with the companies looking for top digital marketing talent. While a good resource to utilize, another excellent resource to implement into your job search are the company websites themselves.

Because of the convenience of having hundreds of job opportunities, if not thousands, on just a couple of websites, too many digital marketing applicants ignore company websites as a great resource to find and gain employment. This is particularly true for smaller companies or elite digital marketing opportunities. Some of these brands will post job openings exclusively on their website. Take the time to look into how your favorite companies and brands advertise job listings and new career opportunities.

The best way to do this is pick out a few dream companies you want to follow, and then sign up for these companies' job alerts. Once you know what opportunities are out there, you can begin customizing a personalized marketing approach to landing a job at these companies you admire and love. Companies like Nike, Apple, and Burberry have career pages on their website, as do many smaller companies you may be interested in also. For this reason, type out your dream company name plus careers in Google to find search results dedicated to the company accepting job applications. Finding your dream job may just be a quick Google search away.

Here is one example of how a job applicant used his digital marketing expertise to land the targeted job of their dreams.

## JOB SEARCHING VS. MARKETING YOURSELF

As digital marketing hopefuls, the truth is your job search should reflect your skills as a marketer. In a job search, after all, you are marketing yourself. John Breneman, expertly illustrates this point in his blog post relaying how he landed his ideal job.

A journalist by trade, John Breneman was laid off by his newspaper. Not content with being unemployed, John put his reporting skills to work and began researching local agencies in his area, looking for ways his expertise could contribute to these agencies. In the process, he began absorbing blogs about marketing, learning new vocabulary and technologies in the process.

Despite these efforts, his hopes to transition from the newsroom to a creative agency focused on marketing was not exactly smooth sailing. However, he had not yet reached out to his favorite agency from the options he had researched. Additionally, he had not added the idea of incorporating inbound marketing strategy into his job search. John decided it was time to reach out to his favorite agency, but not before getting an inbound marketing certification that could be used to develop a clever job pitch.

A former newspaper colleague informed John that he should really take free online video courses to gain certification in inbound marketing. John did so, and he absorbed the many lessons of inbound marketing, but he prioritized one lesson above all else. Namely, he realized he needed to think of prospective employers as a "buyer persona," and that he was pitching himself as the typical product or service that is pitched to a buyer in ordinary inbound marketing.

This revelation led John to build a custom application package on his website that mirrored inbound marketing techniques since his favorite company was in need of a content writer/inbound marketing professional. Instead of sending a standard cover letter and resume, John tailored his approach based on what he learned from his free video courses.

He created unique inbound marketing content with a call to action that led the employers to click over to his personalized landing page online. This, in turn, guided the employers reviewing his application to John's "Thank You" page, which offered enthusiastic endorsements from his former boss. This unique approach led to a job interview in short order. As John puts it, the interview went very well after a good night's sleep and plenty of preparation.

As we have discussed already in the chapter on job interviews, preparation is 80% of the battle when it comes to nailing the job interview.

The lessons to take away from this innovative approach to landing a dream job is that going the extra mile, as John did, is one thing, but it is something else entirely to understand your importance to the job search. Specifically, John needed to educate himself to prepare for the role, and he then needed to market himself in a way that reflected how what he learned and knew how to do made him a great candidate for the job. Now, John landed his dream job based on these efforts, but even if he had not, he would have found a great job eventually. Passion and creativity of this nature will always get your application noticed more quickly than a generic application. Saving your resume from a quick toss into the garbage bin will lead to more interviews, which leads to the increased likelihood of getting that dream job.

## JOB FAIRS AND INDUSTRY EVENTS

For as much as the world has gone digital, job fairs remain a little known and arguably underutilized way into landing a great entry-level digital marketing job. If you are in need of a first break into the field, know that the human connection is a great way to make that first foray into the field.

Plenty of digital marketing agencies and companies in need of digital marketers will participate in local job fairs, so it pays to do your research and find out who will be attending upcoming fairs. Make no mistake about it, companies would not attend these events if they were not an important component of their job recruitment channels.

To pin down where and when events are being held in your area, National Career Fairs is a great resource. This organization outlines a comprehensive listing of events being held throughout the country, which ought to help you target some great digital marketing opportunities. It also pays off to look into whether or not there are local job fairs focused exclusively on digital marketing or digital jobs, such as this job fair for Canadians that was posted on LinkedIn. Resources like these are a great way to put faces to names. Even if you do not land a job through one of these events, you can also leverage them as a great way to begin exchanging business cards and building your digital marketing network, which is another great way to land a job (more on that shortly).

In this way, industry events such as these are great tools to expand your network, leading to a great job in plenty of instances. Expanding digital marketing connections is truly a priceless endeavor, both in person and online. Because of the immediacy of social media influencers, too many digital marketers ignore the value of an in-person connection. These people, particularly if they live nearby, may well become friends, colleagues, and trusted sources to help you solve digital marketing problems.

Trust me, the rapidly changing nature of digital marketing will ensure that you run into problems and dilemmas. Your network will be there to help you when you do, and you will be able to return the favor in kind, given time. These mutually beneficial relationships open doors that lead to opportunities you will not find otherwise. Think of this part of the job search as those "friend of a friend jobs" that do not make it to a job website or company listing.

## THE "WHO YOU KNOW" RESOURCES AND INDUSTRY INFLUENCERS ON SOCIAL MEDIA

In the same way Nike's theme of "Just Do It" is known around the world, "Just Keep Doing" might as well be the motto of the most successful digital marketers. Most digital marketers, particularly the successful ones, have been through a period of immense ups and downs. Shama Hyder's story is no different, given that she wanted a career in social media before it was truly a player in digital marketing.

Shama twice graduated at the top of her class, yet she received a staggering 18 job rejections after receiving her master's degree. Perhaps you can relate, especially if you are trying to break into one of the newer fields of digital marketing. Shama wanted to go into social media marketing before it had truly become an integral component of most businesses' digital marketing efforts. Plenty of businesses, in fact, did not even know what digital marketing was.

Shama did not wait on these businesses. Instead, she bravely ventured out into the world of social media on her own. Shama started a blog as well and also wrote a book as she learned about marketing. As a result, clients eventually came knocking on her door asking for help. Today, Shama Hyder is the successful CEO of Marketing Zen Group, recognized as a digital leader who has been featured in Forbes, Bloomberg, Entrepreneur, and even Cosmo.

Shama is another example of someone who did not land a dream job, but created her own dream job instead. Fortunately, these early pioneers have become industry influencers on LinkedIn and social media. Thanks to their efforts, you can follow the proven paths they have paved for aspiring marketers to follow. You should identify and pay attention to these industry influencers in your field.

If you want to get into analytics-driven marketing, for example, you are going to want to follow an influencer like Avinash Kaushik, who we have talked about in Chapters 3 and 5. If it is SEO you are after, you will want to glean every piece of advice you can from someone like Rand Fishkin, the founder and former CEO of Moz. Of course, female entrepreneurs looking to land a social media marketing position would be wise to pay close attention to Shama Hyder's words of wisdom.

Connecting with these influencers online is a significant opportunity, but do not forget about your in-person network either. This is especially important if your dream job is to work locally. Perhaps you took college courses with a professor who is very connected to the local digital marketing world. Finding local influencers at this level will help ensure you are connected to the right influencers who can contribute to the search for your dream job. Getting national or international digital marketing fame is not for everyone, so know your aspirations, passions, and the difference you want to make in digital marketing. That will help inform you as to the influencers you should be trying to connect with and follow.

## LINKEDIN

We have already discussed the value of social media and influencers, but LinkedIn deserves its own unique mention. While it is true that LinkedIn is a social media platform as well, LinkedIn is important to a job search and is also is simply different from other employment websites. First, just about every company you can imagine is on the platform, allowing you to learn about a company's culture, job expectations, and the like. Further, the platform can help you provide critically important research on specific individuals within the company, which is especially helpful if you land a job interview and know who will be interviewing you.

LinkedIn also enhances its value by providing a LinkedIn Publisher feature allowing you to write op-ed pieces or share some of the things you know in your field. In effect, LinkedIn gives you a unique platform to market your skills and knowledge to prospective employers. Being able to broadcast your knowledge to employers gives you a unique ability to stand out and increase your chances of being hired.

Simply put, LinkedIn must be a part of your resources used in your job search. If you do not yet have LinkedIn membership, make a profile and then come back to finish reading this chapter. It is that important. Why? Let us just look at the essential reasons:

1. Your LinkedIn profile doubles as an online resume that will be viewed by digital marketing professionals, widening the scope of your job search.
2. You can view who has been viewing your profile or is interested in you, allowing you to reach out proactively if you are in a job search. This helps expand your network.
3. LinkedIn helps you target your dream job by following specific company pages and digital marketing groups. This will give you a good feel of the company's culture, helping you assess how to create a targeted pitch that markets yourself in the best light.
4. LinkedIn is yet another jobs board source that provides quality employment opportunities.

David Khim wrote a great article detailing how important LinkedIn was to help him stand out from 437 applicants to get hired at his dream company. David used LinkedIn to find who he would directly report to for the dream job he had his eye on, so he did his research into who his future boss and co-workers would be before he applied. David did this simply by finding the company's LinkedIn page and the list of everyone who worked there. From there, it was an easy path to find his future boss's website and Twitter profile with a simple Google search, helping him learn about her experience and personality. His future boss, Anum Hussain, worked as a content strategist and growth marketer, and David learned everything he could about her. He then researched further into the company culture after this initial research was completed, preparing a targeted cover letter and resume.

Speaking of which, it is difficult to overstate the importance of the cover letter for many LinkedIn jobs. Not only do many jobs require a cover letter, it also gives you the best chance to make a strong and unique first impression as David did. For his part, David crafted a unique cover letter based on all the research he had done, while also including 12 work samples within the cover letter. This can be a helpful technique that spares a future employer from unnecessary busy work while also instantly showcasing why you would be a valuable asset to the company.

With his resume and cover letter in hand, David tweeted out a teaser directly to his hopeful future boss and dream job. David notes that he did not ask permission to send an email in his tweet, he simply informed her that he would be reaching out with an email about the company's digital marketing team. She responded receptively, and David's targeted email based on information gleaned during his research landed him the dream job in a crowded job field of 437 applicants. That, in a nutshell, is the power of leveraging LinkedIn and research into your job search.

## RECRUITERS

If you have yet to land your first job in digital marketing, know that this section will likely not be applicable to your job search. Recruiters are typically looking to help established digital marketers land a new position or help established professionals in a different industry make the transition into digital marketing. Exceptions apply, of course, but as a general rule, recruiters are used by established professionals, first and foremost.

Recruiters, or executive headhunters as they have come to be called, are important because companies increasingly turn to them for help in filling out mid-level digital marketing roles. As such, recruiters are often an instrumental resource in helping professionals take that "next step" in their digital marketing career. Recruiters handle only a small bulk of the digital marketing openings in the industry, but their ability to effectively place talent into desirable jobs based on industry connections and relationships makes them a good option to consider. With the right experience, a recruiter may contact you first, but do not be afraid to reach out and engage recruiters yourself if you are looking to make a career move.

In this book, we have already discussed how there is a talent and skills gap shortage in digital marketing. Well, recruiters are a great tool to help you stand out based on the unique skills you have. These recruiters know the latest tips and trends of the industry, as well as which companies are most in need of your particular digital marketing skills and expertise.

Regarding specific resources online, it is well worth the effort to look into recruiting agencies like digitalgurus.co.uk and onlinedigitaljobs.com. These resources will provide you with agencies that are ideally equipped for placing you into a job role that fits your experience and skillset. Other essential recruitment resources include the highly regarded KingstonStanley, Carter Murray, and Michael Page. Each of these companies provide outstanding recruitment services that place talented people into the right roles.

## DO NOT FORGET ABOUT STARTUPS

During your job search, you are going to frequently run into job posting centered around the digital marketing needs of agencies and brands. While these are great digital marketing jobs, remember that startups have a strong need for talented digital marketers as well.

Startups, in many cases, are working with the most cutting-edge products and technologies in the industry, making these positions a great landing spot for anyone who values behind-the-scenes and cutting-edge work. Some startups are far from small-time players when it comes to the products and technologies they offer to their clients, and this carries over into employment.

What kind of startups are worth considering? Realistically, you should consider any startup that excites you and is in serious need of digital marketing help. Whether that help is social media outreach, eCommerce expertise, or SEO will inform whether they are the right fit for your skills, but rest assured there are plenty of opportunities out there.

## PUTTING IT ALL TOGETHER

Putting these tools together—and putting them to work for your job search—should give you all the inspiration and information needed to take the steps toward your dream job. Once you have landed that dream job, be sure to come back and re-read my words on what you should next.

Answering the "What next?" question is a critical step in your professional growth, but it will also help you explore who you are personally. When you land the dream job, do not let thoughts of doubt or pessimism affect you. It is only natural that, for some people, landing a dream job will trigger a sense of worry that you may "ruin a good thing." No, you landed your dream job for a reason. Your employer believes in you, and you believe in yourself as well, or you would not have applied for the dream job in the first place. Remind yourself of this fact, constantly.

At the same time, do not enter in overly confident based on past successes. Digital marketing has a way of humbling even the proudest success stories, based on the frequent change and the constant learning that comes along with the change. Enter your new job with humility, gratefulness and a "blank slate" approach. Do not ignore past successes—or past failures, for that matter—because relying on this experience and the lessons learned makes you a better digital marketer. With that said, digital marketing is an innovative approach, so look at your new position with fresh eyes and an approach that asks how you can create solutions that drive value for your brand, agency, vendor, etc. If you are in business for yourself as a digital marketing entrepreneur, these lessons are just as valuable.

Maintain an open mind and a willingness to try new things. In essence, this means you should never stop "doing" in the field of digital marketing. Few jobs reward "doing" quite like digital marketing, and thanks to the lessons you will learn that can be applied to your job and life. As Seth Godin puts it, "marketing is no longer about the stuff that you make, but about the stories you tell." Make your story one of commitment to staying passionate and never settling for anything less than pursuing your dream job and using it to make a positive difference in the lives of others.

Jeff Bezos, the founder of Amazon, is fond of saying, "You don't choose your passions. Your passions choose you." I can only speak for myself and say that these sentiments ring true. Digital marketing chose me, and I have a suspicion it chose you as well since you are reading these words. The great thing about this dynamic is that you now have the freedom to take your passion and run with it, until you have found the career that makes the long hours and hard work worth it.

INTENTIONALLY LEFT BLANK

# 12

////////////////////////////////////////////////////////

## WHY AGENCY LIFE IS A GREAT ENTRY POINT INTO DIGITAL MARKETING

To instantly understand how uniquely suited digital marketing agencies are for giving a digital marketer their first job in the industry, simply look at the profiles of senior leadership positions in digital marketing. Some of the industry's top executives got their start working their way up at a digital marketing agency.

Josh Steimle, named one of the 50 online marketing influencers to watch in 2016, serves as a great example of this fact. For those just getting started in digital marketing, they may be more familiar with Josh's work as the successful author of *Chief Marketing Officers at Work*. Before Josh was a successful author and before he became CEO at MWI, he started out at the ground level by creating his own agency as a college student. MWI is an employer of countless other aspiring digital marketers starting out as young college graduates.

Plenty of digital marketers may want to learn the ropes of the industry with a stable agency job before branching out and trying to start their own agency. Not only is this understandable, it is also a great way to get firsthand industry experience that helps you in whatever digital marketing career you view as the ultimate "dream job." This is true whether you are in college and in need of an internship or if you are a new graduate looking for your first entry-level role.

Eric Siu, CEO of the digital marketing agency Single Grain, advises young college undergraduates that working at an agency is a great way to stand out from the crowd during the early stages of a career. According to Siu, "internships at work experience during college are a great way to add practical skills as well as credentials to your resume...if you want to go into Internet marketing, look for an internship with an agency that offers Internet marketing services." The takeaway from Siu's advice is that job hopefuls should look for a digital marketing agency that offers hands-on experience that will translate into valuable experience for your ideal marketing career.

Again, if you are looking for success stories, just spend 10 minutes researching top executives and managing directors on LinkedIn. You will soon see that time spent at an agency was a critically important stepping stone toward greater digital marketing success.

## FINDING THE RIGHT AGENCY POSITION

A great piece of writing from Digital Marketing Institute sheds light on how to know whether working at an agency is a good fit for you. The article begins by addressing how agency life can be uniquely suitable for creative minds. Agency life is a perfect fit for creative people who thrive on a fast pace and a constant flow of new projects, while keeping the agency's big ideas in mind. The reason for this is that agencies are in the business of pitching their ideas to brands who are looking to buy into fresh, innovative, and creative marketing approaches.

Entry-level positions at a digital marketing agency often involve creating these ideas and working within a team-based environment to brainstorm/ run a wide range of marketing campaigns. One day you may be pitching an idea for a fashion brand's social media outreach, and the next week you may be helping a brand implement a redesigned eCommerce storefront. In short, if you like solving constant new challenges regularly, agency life is a great place to hone your marketing skillset.

While agency employment is a natural fit for creative people, it is also a great fit for anyone with an entrepreneurial spirit who is thinking of starting an agency of their own someday. The reason for this is that agency life provides unique insights into the business side of digital marketing. Derek Nelson, a partner and creative director at Clique Studios, recently wrote a piece about the importance of starting out at a digital agency. Nelson specifically points out how beneficial agency life is for an entrepreneurial self-starter since agency work forces young marketers to discover their talents by exposing them to a variety of opportunities and digital marketing roles. These lessons will help the young marketer discern what makes them excel and where they thrive. In effect, agency life helps you find your niche by throwing concepts at you very quickly.

Of course, this fast pace means digital marketing is not for everyone. While you may be passionate about digital marketing, you may have a personality that prefers a more relaxed pace. In that case, you may prefer to work on the client side at a brand or look for employment client-side at a brand that resonates with you. These opportunities are also exciting but provide more long-term job stability and consistency in the roles performed.

If the rapid pace gets your gears turning with the possibilities, know that the lessons learned from time at an agency is invaluably helpful. Some of the key lessons you will take away from time working at an agency include the following:

* Enhanced Interpersonal Skills after Working Closely with a Wide Range of Clients
* The Ability to Problem Solve Creatively in a Time-Efficient Manner (Since Typical Agencies Are Paid by the Hour, You Will Be Expected to Make Good Use of Time and Honestly Record How Much Time You Spend On Various Tasks)
* Multi-Tasking Skills That Will Be Helpful for Any Entrepreneur Who Starts Their Own Agency or a Similar Endeavor
* The Ability to Sharpen Your Communication Skills When Pitching Ideas or Solutions To Agency Clients

# MOVING UP THE CORPORATE LADDER

A key element of agency life is that turnover is quite high, meaning that terminations, layoffs, and people choosing to move on to a new opportunity is just part of the business model. Knowing this in advance is in your best interests since you can prepare accordingly. For the ambitious and skilled digital marketer, this reality provides the opportunity for rapid career advancement. Succeeding in digital marketing largely depends on resilience, passion, creativity and being willing to adapt and positively respond to change. Few jobs teach these skills quite like working in an agency, whether you make it to managing director or get laid off after 18 months of employment.

Finally, agency life has another crucial benefit that is discussed too infrequently in the digital marketing industry. Let us assume that having a specialized skill and working your hardest is ultimately unable to save your job at the agency. First of all, it happens. But—and more importantly—second of all, there are many other agencies out there that would love to hire you. If you were either a temp contract or a full-time employee of an agency, the skills you learned will likely be highly desired by another agency.

Moving from agency to agency is a common career path for digital marketers who are first learning the profession. Not only is this a great way to advance your career with rapid promotions in a highly volatile digital marketing field, it also exposes you to several different digital marketing business models and strategies. Each of these lessons will give you a great roadmap on what does and does not work if you ever choose to start your own agency one day as many of the greatest digital influencers have done. In fact, these lessons are so beneficial that plenty of agency employees seek to make moves to other agencies with the express purpose of obtaining new digital marketing skills.

With that said, do not treat this volatility as an excuse to job hop, acting as though the rollercoaster ride will never come to an end. Employers and agencies do talk to one another regularly, particularly when it comes to asking about previous employees. While the industry is large and the agency opportunities are immense, the executive community is surprisingly tight-knit and well-connected. Agencies know when contractions happen, when they have not happened, and when candidates are changing jobs for the right reasons. If you get an agency job and want to change employers, know why and make it clear when interviewed exactly why the new position tracks with your career goals.

For a great example of how agency life prepares you for digital marketing success, take a look at the legacy roadmap paved by Rohit Bhargava. Today, Bhargava is best known as the CEO and founder of Influential Marketing Group and the bestselling author of five digital marketing books. Of course, Bhargava did not just magically become a CEO and bestselling author without years of digital marketing experience. For Bhargava, cutting his teeth in digital marketing with more than 10 years of digital agency experience was key to his success.

After spending 15 years in agencies before making his rise to CEO, Georgetown professor and bestselling author, Bhargava has accumulated a world of insight into the world of digital agencies. One of the key lessons an agency can teach digital marketers is how to understand the true needs of a client, even if that is not what the client is asking for. If there is only one lesson you take away from your time in an agency, make it this one. Understand a client's true needs, no matter what, and you are well on your way to success in both agency life and whatever comes next.

Clients are demanding and want results, but they may not know the best way to get there. You are the digital marketing expert, after all. In this way, even if you are an entry-level marketer, start thinking of yourself and the client as partners on a journey together. Figure out what they need, and find a way to effectively deliver that solution with innovative pitches and compelling ideas. Do that, and digital marketing success should come naturally in the same way it has for Bhargava. Of course, that is not to say it will come instantly.

Bhargava put in long hours and well over a decade of work into agency life before branching out as an entrepreneur, respected academic and renowned author. Take no shortcuts and understand your clients, learning transferable skills for any area of digital marketing in the process.

# WHY DIGITAL MARKETING AGENCIES BOTH ARE AND ARE NOT YOUR TRADITIONAL AGENCY

When looking for a digital marketing job at an agency, you may soon realize there is plenty of overlap between digital and traditional agencies. You will especially notice this if you are making a career transition from a traditional advertising firm. The same job functions and titles tend to make an appearance at both, such as the following:

* Creative Directors
* Account Management Roles
* Media Positions
* Planning Departments

With that said, there are notable differences once you look past these surface-level similarities. Traditional ad agencies are best thought of as brand focused, working on making sure ideas will sell products. This philosophy is what leads to memorable advertisements or catchy slogans like Nike's "Just Do It." The clever headlines and idea-based marketing usually is paired with high production values, meaning advertising awards are highly coveted by these agencies. Traditional agency advertisements appear most regularly in TV, print, radio, and on the Web. The employees who work together on these ads are copywriters, designers, account managers, and product departments.

Conversely, digital agencies have the overarching philosophy to be driven by effective content and data. Awards are not the important thing for the digital agency, but results are. Since results are of the utmost importance, the digital marketer is driven by metrics and measurables, no matter whether the marketer works on PPC, social media marketing, or SEO. The tools are varied for the digital marketer, but websites, mobile apps, SEO, content marketing, email marketing, social media, PPC, and analytics are all tools of the trade. In effect, basically everything this book has discussed guides the digital agency's task to focus on reaching the consumer on all sorts of screens and digital devices.

In this way, digital agencies are a better choice for a digital marketer who wants to remain exclusively in the digital marketing world. Agencies will operate with the latest technology to maintain a competitive advantage or to keep up with competitors, meaning agency employees, should they end up leaving the agency, will walk out the door with some of the latest industry training. These benefits are invaluable and are easily put to use immediately in the constant change reality of digital marketing.

No matter where you land after agency life, whether with another agency, client-side or starting an entrepreneurial journey of your own, the lessons learned should prove immensely helpful. These are a few of the job titles you will come across if you pursue employment at a digital marketing agency.

## LOOKING BEYOND AGENCY LIFE

Nothing in life lasts forever, and by now you know this truth is particularly applicable to agency life. Fortunately, working as a digital marketer is the most entrepreneurial job in marketing, so there are many opportunities beyond agency life. This is unsurprising when you look at a list of the most influential marketing influencers, some of whom—like Gary Vaynerchuk and Neil Patel—never worked at an agency at all. Rest assured you will find plenty of entrepreneurs who regularly appear on the "who's who" and industry influencer lists who never worked at an agency. Still, you will also find plenty who used their time at an agency to spread their wings and to become successful entrepreneurs.

Never think that starting your career in an agency, whether it is small or large, confines you to agency employment for the remainder of your career. Digital marketing changes too rapidly and evolves too quickly for you to be held down to a specific type of employment. Instead, those with an entrepreneurial spirit should look at agency employment as a great step towards achieving all your entrepreneurial goals and dreams.

Whether you specialize in social media marketing, SEO, or any other desirable marketing field, being able to see agency life from the inside will teach you lasting lessons you can use to start your own agency or entrepreneurial vision.

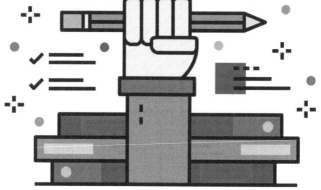

# 13

//////////////////////////////////////////////////////////

# A CAREER IN DIGITAL MARKETING IS A LIFELONG EDUCATIONAL PURSUIT

## WHAT YOU WILL LEARN IN THIS CHAPTER:

* Why University and College Courses Are Great Educational Options for Digital Marketing Success
* Which Low-Cost and Online Training Courses Are Known to Deliver the Best Results
* The Free Online Resources to Meaningfully Advance Your Knowledge Without Spending a Thing Other Than Your Time
* The Immense Value of Marketing Associations and Digital Marketing Groups
* The Secret to Sustaining Digital Marketing Success

Do a Google search for "digital marketing schools," and you will quickly find yourself inundated with choices. Fortunately, there are now a wealth of options when it comes to digital marketing education. This was not always the case, and self-teaching was essential in the earliest days of digital marketing. Today, there are many educators who are ready, willing, and able to pass forward what they have learned. This book itself is a testament to just that.

However, merely having options is not entirely helpful if a digital marketing hopeful is overwhelmed and does not know where to begin. When you are new to a respective field, even diligent research is not sufficient for finding the best educational programs and resources. You are new to the industry, after all, so what may look like a great program to a digital marketing newcomer may in actuality be a middling resource. This chapter aims to eliminate the guesswork surrounding your educational options, empowering you to find great resources that will further your digital marketing career ambitions.

## UNIVERSITY AND COLLEGE DEGREE PROGRAMS

### 1. Certifications

**Google Adwords Fundamentals (Search, Display, Video, Mobile, & Shopping Advertising)**
Taught by: Google
Price: Free
Study Method: Online, Self-paced
Duration: 2 Weeks, Part-time
Skill Level: Beginner, Intermediate
https://www.google.com/partners/#p_adwordscertification

**Google Analytics (Beginners & Advances)**
Taught by: Google
Price: Free
Study Method: Online, Self-paced
Duration: 2 Weeks, Part-time
Skill Level: Beginner, Intermediate
https://www.google.com/partners/#p_analyticscertification

## Mobile Sites
Taught by: Google
Price: Free
Study Method: Online, self-paced
Duration: 2 Weeks, Part-time
Skill Level: Beginner, Intermediate
https://www.google.com/partners/#p_mobilesitescertification

## Mobile App Marketing
Taught by: Google
Price: Free
Study Method: Online, Self-paced
Duration: 2 Weeks, Part-time
Skill Level: Beginner, Intermediate
https://www.udacity.com/course/app-marketing--ud719

## Digital Marketing NanoDegree
Taught by: Udacity
Price: $999
Study Method: Online
Duration: Three Months
Skill Level: Beginner, Intermediate
https://www.udacity.com/course/digital-marketing-nanodegree--nd018

## Digital Marketing Certified Associate Training Course
Taught by: Market Motive
Price: $499
Study Method: Online, Self-paced
Skill Level: Beginner, Intermediate
Duration: 1 Year
http://www.marketmotive.com/digital-marketing-certification-train-ing-courses/

## 2. Diploma

**Diploma in Digital Marketing**
Taught by: MMC Learning
Accreditation: Chartered Institute of Marketing (CIM)
Price: £1,847
Study Method: Online
Duration: 9 to 12 Months, 4 Hours per Week
Skill Level: Beginner, Intermediate
http://www.mmclearning.com/wp-content/uploads/files/MMC-Certificate-in-Professional-Marketing-Module-2-Integrated-Communications.pdf

**Professional Diploma in Digital Marketing**
Taught by: Digital Marketing Institute
Accreditation: SQA Level 8 Scottish Credit and Qualifications Framework (SCQF)
Price: $1,965
Study Method: Online
Duration: 30 Hours
Skill Level: Beginner
https://digitalmarketinginstitute.com/students/courses/professional-diploma-in-digital-marketing

**Professional Diploma in Digital Marketing**
Taught by: IDM - The Institute of Direct & Digital Marketing
Accreditation: UK Level 6 Qualification, Equal to Bachelor's Degree Level
Price: £2575
Study Method: Online
Duration: 12 Months
Skill Level: Beginner
https://www.theidm.com/marketing-qualifications/professional-diplomas/idm-professional-diploma-in-digital-marketing

**Diploma of Business (Digital Marketing)**
Taught by: The Left Bank
Accreditation: ASQA (Australian Skills Quality Authority)
Price: $8850
Study Method: Online
Duration: 2 Years (Part-time), 1 Year (Full-time)
Skill Level: Beginner
http://www.theleftbank.edu.au/digital-marketing-courses/diploma-of-digital-marketing/

**New York University Advanced Diploma in Digital Marketing**
Taught by: New York University (NYU)
Accreditation: New York State Education Department (NYSED)
Price: $2,750
Study method: Online
Duration: 1 Year
Skill Level: Advanced

## 3. Bachelors

**Bachelor of Science in Business Administration - Digital Marketing**
Taught by: Colorado Technical University
Accreditation: Accreditation Council for Business Schools and Programs (ACBSP)
Price: $58,500
Study Method: Online
Duration: 4 Years
Skill Level: Advanced
http://www.coloradotech.edu/degrees/bachelors/business/digital-marketing

**Bachelor of Science in Digital Marketing**
Taught by: New England College of Business
Accreditation: New England Association of Schools and Colleges (NEASC)
Price: $58,200
Study Method: Online
Duration: 4 Years
Skill Level: Advanced

https://www.necb.edu/undergraduate-course-descriptions/

## B.S. Degree in Digital Marketing Technology – Online
Taught by: University of Wisconsin-Stout
Accreditation: Wisconsin Department of Public Instruction
Price: $40,080
Study Method: Online
Duration: 4 Years
Skill Level: Advanced
http://www.uwstout.edu/programs/bsdmt-online/

## Bachelor of Arts in eMarketing
Taught by: Ashford University
Accreditation: WASC Senior College and University Commission (WS-CUC)
Price: $54,240
Study Method: Online
Duration: 4 Years
Skill Level: Advanced
https://www.ashford.edu/online-degrees/business/bachelor-of-arts-emarketing

## Bachelor of Science in Internet Marketing
Taught by: Full Sail University
Accreditation: Accrediting Commission of Career Schools and Colleges (ACCSC)
Price: $54,000
Study Method: Online
Duration: 4 Years
Skill Level: Advanced
https://www.fullsail.edu/degrees/internet-marketing-bachelor

## 4. Post Graduate & Masters

## Postgraduate Diploma in Digital Marketing
Taught by: Digital Marketing Institute
Accreditation: SQA Level 11 Scottish Credit and Qualifications Framework (SCQF)

Price: $5365
Study Method: Online
Duration: 1 Year (Part-time)
Skill Level: Advanced
https://digitalmarketinginstitute.com/students/courses/postgraduate-diploma-in-digital-marketing

**Masters in Digital Marketing**
Taught by: Digital Marketing Institute
Accreditation: SQA Level 11 Scottish Credit and Qualifications Framework (SCQF)
Price: $10,735
Study Method: Online
Duration: 2 years (Part-time)
Skill Level: Intermediate, Advanced
https://digitalmarketinginstitute.com/students/courses/masters-in-digital-marketing

**Masters in Digital Marketing & Strategy**
Taught by: University of Florida
Accreditation: Southern Association of Colleges and Schools Commission on Colleges (SACSCOC)
Price: $17,000-34,000 (In-state/Out-of-State Students)
Study Method: Online
Duration: 2 Years (Full-time)
Skill Level: Advanced
http://onlinemasters.jou.ufl.edu/digital-strategy/

**Digital Marketing (PgCert -> PgDip -> MSc)**
Taught by: Salford University UK
Accreditation: ASQA (Australian Skills Quality Authority)
Price: £8,500 Full-time and £13,500 Full-time International for PGCert, PG-Dip and MSc
Study Method: Online
Duration: 2 Years (Part-time), 1 Year (Full-time)
Skill Level: Advanced
http://www.salford.ac.uk/pgt-courses/digital-marketing

**Digital Marketing Leadership (PgCert -> PgDip -> MSc)**
Taught by: University of Aberdeen
Price: PgCert: £3250 PgDiploma: £3250 MSc: £3250 Total fee is £9750
Study Method: Online
Duration: 2 to 4 Years
Skill Level: Advanced
https://www.abdn.ac.uk/study/postgraduate-taught/degree-pro-grammes/52/digital-marketing-leadership/

# BOOKS TO ADD TO YOUR DIGITAL MARKETING COLLECTION

No matter which field of digital marketing you are looking to go into, it will help you to read books dedicated to helping you excel in those fields. To point you in the right direction, I have included what I have found to be the top books to read for each field of digital marketing addressed in this book.

## ECOMMERCE

*What Customers Crave* by Nicholas Webb
  * The book helps eCommerce marketers rethink key aspects of this field.
  * It teaches that getting to know customers is centrally important for sustained success.
  * The book informs marketers how to create better customer experience.

Online stores and eCommerce marketers simply cannot succeed without knowing how to appeal to their customers. Nicholas Webb drives this point home with emphasis in this influential book. Rethinking all aspects of customer service and the customer's experience will be what sets the best eCommerce marketers apart, helping online storefronts boost conversion rates in the process.

## MOBILE MARKETING

*The New Rules of Marketing an♦ PR: How to Use Social Me♦ia, Online Vi♦eo, Mobile Applications, Blogs, News Releases, an♦ Viral Marketing to Reach Buyers Directly* by David Meerman Scott
  * This book teaches what is new in the world of mobile marketing.

- While staying true to what is new, the book still emphasizes certain unchanging aspects of digital marketing.
- The book is packed with real-world examples designed to take your mobile marketing efforts to the next level.

With this book, David Meerman Scott is helping mobile marketers adapt to the regular innovations within their field. The book has plenty of wisdom applicable to other digital marketing fields as well, which is important since mobile marketing efforts often depend on other areas of marketing expertise. Best of all, the book is loaded with real-world examples and studies that drive home the most important aspects of the book. Most importantly, Scott shows his readers that gaining publicity is the key to mobile marketing and mobile app success.

## SOCIAL MEDIA MARKETING

*Crush It!* by Gary Vaynerchuk
- The book provides basic information that gives you excellent foundational knowledge.
- It inspires you to take action like few other digital marketing books.
- It teaches how to leverage the art of narrative on social media.

Few digital marketing pros have the passion of Vaynerchuk, and his inspirational masterclass gives the budding social media marketer all the inspiration they could ever need. On top of the inspiration, Gary takes readers on a journey into key foundational aspects of social media marketing, while teaching the art of telling a good story. Brands only succeed via social media when they tell a great story, and this lesson is drilled home by one of digital marketing's master storytellers.

## DIGITAL ANALYTICS

*Analytics 2.0* by Avinash Kaushik
- In-depth analytics analysis helps you hone and sharpen your analytics ability.
- Avinash tackles some of the toughest challenges in analytics, and the reader is sure to benefit.
- The book takes high-brow topics and condenses it for an easy read.

As one of my greatest digital marketing influences, I cannot recommend

Avinash Kaushik's masterclass on digital analytics highly enough. He truly takes on the tough subjects and gets into the fine details of analytics, helping the aspiring analytics expert hone their abilities purely by reading. Kaushik achieves this by taking what ought to be difficult to digest subjects and condensing them into an easy, enjoyable, and immensely understandable read.

## SEM AND DISPLAY ADVERTISING

*Search Engine Marketing, Inc.: Driving Search Traffic to Your Company's Website* by Mike Moran
  * This book is a leading and practical guide for driving value from search.
  * It is already on its third edition since Moran is committed to staying on top of the SEM changes.
  * Beginners will appreciate the straightforward explanations and intermediate marketers will love the book for its depth.

Mike Moran's latest edition of his book has updated some of the most important changes to SEM, which only cements his book as a seminal work on SEM and display advertising. Already on its third edition, the latest text takes a complete approach to both organic and paid search, ensuring there are nuggets of wisdom to be had for all SEM professionals. The book is easy to pick up and engage with for new SEM marketers and more experienced marketers alike, making it an easy recommendation no matter how far along you are in your career.

## EMAIL MARKETING

*Email Marketing Demystifie*  by Matthew Paulson
  * The book hones in on the latest shifts in SEO.
  * It includes some of the best insights from his influential Moz blog.
  * It tells you what it takes to remain a cutting-edge force in SEO.

Email marketing is all about reaching the right targeted leads and at the right time. Paulson's book teaches readers how to do just that. As the book title implies, he expertly demystifies some of the more complex aspects of email marketing, such as how to build massive email lists or realizing an excellent ROI. Along the way, he paints a picture with quality stories and proven research that makes the book as informative as it is relatable, just like quality email marketing.

## DIGITAL MARKETING SALES

*Selling the Invisible* by Harry Beckwith
- The book focuses on creating an emotional connection to sell the invisible in a digital world.
- It explores the psychology behind what compels consumers to purchase.
- It emphasizes making what people can see count as a digital salesperson.

The salesman has had a long and storied history throughout the world, but the move to digital has shaken things up. For Harry Beckwith, this new-found reality simply presents new opportunities for creating an emotional connection with others. Beckwith helpfully navigates the reader through the psychology of consumer behavior, making you a more effective salesperson in the process. Lessons that will be learned include emphasizing what people can see and how any business or brand can benefit from timeless sales techniques.

## SEO

*SEO: Insights from the Moz Blog* by Rand Fishkin
- The book hones in on the latest shifts in SEO.
- It includes some of the best insights from his influential Moz blog.
- It tells you what it takes to remain a cutting-edge force in SEO.

Finally, I would be remiss not to include Rand Fishkin as well. Rand is another digital marketing influence who inspires me to do my best work. Fishkin, perhaps best known for his work on the Moz blog, shares his most important insights from successfully running Moz. The book, Inbound Marketing and SEO: Insights from the Moz Blog, is a great snapshot into the thought process of what it takes to remain cutting-edge in a constantly changing field. Moz is inherently focused on the constant shifts of SEO and how that affects inbound marketing and SEO, but the general principles discussed by Fishkin are applicable to all aspects of digital marketing.

# COMMITTING TO LIFELONG LEARNING IS THE BEST WAY TO ENJOY SUSTAINED SUCCESS AS A DIGITAL MARKETER

I hope that with my book, these additional readings and the educational resources listed in this chapter, you will have all the tools you need to succeed in today's digital marketing landscape. But, as I have reminded at several points in this book, mastering today's digital marketing is just the beginning. Today's digital marketing landscape will not look like tomorrow's, and the digital marketing of tomorrow will ultimately innovate and evolve as well.

The truth about mastering the resources provided herein is that you will eventually need additional training and education. Such is life as a digital marketer. With that said, the skills you learn today will give you a solid foundation that makes learning future concepts easier since future changes will largely be evolutions of what you already learned and know. It is still essential to always keep in mind that current best practices in digital marketing will only last for so long.

This is why I also strongly recommend digital marketing books that inspire you to challenge yourself and commit to lifelong learning. Technical knowledge is one thing, but loving knowledge simply for learning's sake is the best way to enjoy sustained success as a digital marketer. This assertion has proved true for me and every other digital marketer I know, both personally and professionally.

This book is my way of paying this knowledge forward, and it is my hope that you take away hundreds, if not thousands, of valuable lessons from this book. However, if you take away only a single lesson, make it this: Be a lifelong learner in whatever you wish to pursue and work hard. Success will follow in short order.

INTENTIONALLY LEFT BLANK

# Glossary

**A**

AdSense - Google's AdSense is a pay-per-click form of advertising that lets bloggers and websites generate income from website traffic. Site owners choose the ads to be hosted, and AdSense pays owners whenever the ad is clicked.

AdWords - Google's search engine marketing (SEM) program that provides pay-per-click advertising for businesses. The business sets an advertising budget and pays only when people click on their advertisements.

Algorithm - A process or ruleset that is followed in computer calculations. Algorithms are used in technical code, search engines, and similarly important facets of digital marketing.

Anchor Text   Text that is displayed in a clickable hyperlink that is not the URL address. For example, clicking on the text of a hyperlink stating "Facebook's website" can take you to the website itself.

**B**

Backlink - A link directed to your site from another website. Also known as an inbound link.

Banner Ad - An advertisement that uses an image or animation file embedded within a webpage for advertising efforts. This ad may contain a link to another site or product.

Blog - Shorthand for weblog, a blog is a self-publishing website that typically records and categorizes content updates by both date and topic. Posts typically appear in reverse chronological order and can be created by the site's owner (known as a "blogger") or several authors who update the blog's content.

Broken Links - The term used for links to pages that either no longer exist or have moved to a new URL without redirection. Broken links frequently result in a 404 error that alerts visitors to the fact that the link is broken.

## C

Click-through Rate (CTR) - Percentage of visitors who click on a link after seeing it. This rate can be used for email messages, sponsored ads, etc.

Content - The driving force of digital marketing, content can refer to any material that is published online for the consumption of a target audience. Text, image, video, audio, and other material can all be categorized as content.

Conversion - The term used for when a target audience visitor performs the action a brand desires. Subscribing to an email newsletter, making a purchase, or downloading a file can all be categorized as conversion if that is the end result a brand wants to achieve.

Cost-Per-Click - A form of payment for targeted traffic that is offered by prominent websites like Facebook and Google. Brands have a specific budget in mind and agree to pay a set amount for every click resulting from targeted traffic.

Crawler - Some search engines automatically index a page and then visit pages that the indexed page links to, leading to very fast indexing. These automatic indexing functions are known as crawlers/"spiders."

## D

Digital Marketing - A catch-all term for marketing products and services by using digital technologies. As such, digital marketing primarily refers to internet-based marketing efforts.

Directory - A helpful index of websites that compile listings by hand rather than using a crawler. The best directory sites should be updated regularly with the use of structured guidelines.

DNS - A term that stands for "Domain Name Service," "Domain Name System," and "Domain Name Server." This name service allows computers to utilize letters and numbers that make up a domain name rather than an IP address.

# E

Email - Messages sent over a network from one computer user to another. Gmail is one example of a popular email platform.

Email Marketing -The method of targeting customers through email, which is an evolution of traditional marketing efforts through direct mail.

# F

Facebook - A leading social network that plays an important role in social media marketing and other essential aspects of digital marketing.

Flash - Video software created by Adobe that creates graphic animations that can be used in digital marketing efforts.

# G

Graphical Search Inventory - Banner advertisements and images that are connected to precise search terms on the search engine that are displayed once specific search terms are used.

Groups - Smaller communities within social networking sites dedicated to specific ideas or areas of interest. For digital marketing job seekers, LinkedIn groups can be particularly helpful.

# H

H-Tags - Shorthand for "header tags," H-Tags are page elements that represent different sizes of HTML headings, ranging from H1 (largest) to H6 (smallest). For search engine optimization and reader benefit, header tags should incorporate keywords whenever possible.

Hashtag - A # symbol placed in front of a word or phrase for posts that are tagged on Twitter. This symbol is used to group tweets to help users keep up with the latest topics and trending discussions.

HTML - Shorthand for hypertext markup language, HTML is the text-based language used when creating a website.

Hyperlink - Also known as a link, hyperlinks are words or phrases that are clicked on and then take a visitor to a new webpage. Hyperlinks can take visitors to a different page on the same website or a new website altogether.

## I

Index - The search engine's collection of data and websites. Also referred to as a "search index."

Inbound Link - Also known as a backlink, an inbound link is a link that directs to your website from another site. Social media marketing benefits from collecting quality links from other websites.

Instagram - A popular photo sharing social network that has been used to great effect in clever digital marketing campaigns.

IP Address - A series of numbers and periods that provide a unique identifying address for every internet user.

## J

Java - Programming language that operates independently of platforms, allowing it to run on multiple operating systems and computers.

JavaScript - A scripting language that integrated with HTML and is used on websites. It is beloved for its simplicity, although its simplicity makes it less powerful when compared to Java.

## K

Keyword - A term that a search engine user enters into the search engine. Also can refer to the terms a website targets to rise in search engine rankings during SEO marketing efforts.

Keyword Density - The proportion of keywords in relation to the total number of words used in a blog post or website's page copy.

## L

Landing Page - A commonly visited page a visitor is meant to "land on" after clicking a search engine advertisement or clicking a newsletter link. These pages are typically designed with user conversion in mind.

Link - See "Hyperlink."

Link Farm - Websites that have fallen out of favor with search engines today. These websites list a large number of links, albeit without structure or categorization. Engaging with a link farm site in the current SEO climate leads to ranking penalties, making link farm association undesirable.

Link Text - See "Anchor Text."

LinkedIn - A social networking platform for business professionals that lets users connect with one another, share updates, take part in chats, and join groups.

## M

Meta-Tags - Information found in HTML page headers that include title, description, and keyword tags to improve SEO results. While meta-tags are not as important today as in years past, they are still a useful tool for improving search rankings.

Meta-Description - This tag is located in heading source code and provides a helpful description of the webpage itself. A good meta-description will provide valuable information to search engine users who find the page listing while also helping the search engine categorize the page efficiently.

Microblog - Microblogs let users share short, succinct status updates, posts, and information. The most famous microblog is Twitter, which combines microblogging practices with social networking functionality.

# N

Natural Listings - See "Organic Listings."

# O

Organic Listings - Also referred to as "natural listings," these are non-purchased search engine results. Instead, the search engine algorithm sorts results based on the quality of the listed pages. Google, for example, places sponsored ads related to search terms with a separate color and background before placing the non-paid listing results.

Outbound Links - Links on a webpage that link to external webpages.

# P

Paid Listings - Listings that are sold to advertisers for a fee, making the listings a paid placement of sorts. Pay-per-click is a paid listing.

Pay-Per-Click (PPC) - Paid search marketing that puts an advertise either above or alongside the organic, free search listings. Obtaining a high position among PPC ads is based on the owner's "bid," which can lead to a bidding war for desired listing pages.

Peer to Peer (P2P) - Interaction between two or more individuals on a social network. Viral content typically results from heavily shared P2P content.

Position - Synonymous with "rank" for search engine listings.

Profile - A user's individual page on a social network that is created to connect with others on the network and share updates. The profile may provide basic user information, personal updates/posts, and links to the profile's connections and friends.

# Q

Query - Search terms entered into the engine by a user.

# R

Ranking - A website listing's placement in search engine results. Saying that a listing has a "high ranking" for a keyword signifies that the page is more visible to search engine users than lower ranking listings.

Reciprocal Link - Linking to a website that "reciprocates" with a backlink. The mutual nature of such linking usually is created by correspondence and agreement between sites that will receive a mutual benefit from the reciprocity. This strategy can be abused in a process known as link farming, which leads to search engine ranking penalties. See "Link Farm."

Results Page - The results displayed after a user's query is input into the search engine. Also known as a "Search Engine Results Page (SERP)."

Return on Investment (ROI) - The percentage of profit that results from a digital marketing strategy based on the amount of money spent on marketing.

# S

Search Engine - Websites that let users search for information by using keywords and queries.

Search Engine Marketing (SEM) - Refers to paid search activities, usually designed to contrast with the organic marketing efforts of SEO. SEM can, however, refer to both paid and organic search marketing efforts.

Search Engine Optimization (SEO) - Using web analysis and content/structural changes to both improve rankings results on search engine pages and improve the website experience for users.

Search Term - The exact word or phrase entered into a search engine, also referred to as a query.

Social Media - Refers to all media, tools, and networks that let users communicate with one another online and create content. Examples of social media include social networks, blogs, file-hosting, and more.

Social Network - An online community that lets members share content and interact.

Spam - An email marketing concept, spam refers to messages considered to be unsolicited commercial offers by email providers or their users.

## T

Tag - Tags are keywords that are attached to blog posts, tweets, and more. A tag helps categorize the content appropriately.

Title Tag - Meta-data that categorizes webpages by their title. Most search engine algorithms have traditionally used this form of tag to help categorize pages.

Twitter - The most famous microblogging platform (See "Microblog"). The social network lets users create individual profiles, share updates, and interact with other users on the platform.

## U

Unique Visitor - A statistic designed to track visitors to a website by counting each individual visitor only once in a given time period, even if they make multiple visits.

URL - Shorthand for Uniform Resource Locator, the URL is a sequence of numbers and letters that are separated by periods and slashes for all pages on the internet. A webpage address must be written in this way to be found online.

User-Generated Content (UGC) - UGC is any content created by a member of the website audience that can be shared on the website or distributed more widely across the Web.

## V

Voice Over internet Protocol (VOIP) - Technology that makes it possible for users to make phone calls over PC with an Internet connection or Wi-

Fi connected mobile device. Skype is the most well-known VOIP provider.

# W

Webinar - A Web-based seminar that contains audio and/or video. This form of seminar is usually used to provide information and educational value, and the same holds true for valuable digital marketing webinars.

Wiki - Collections of pages online that are editable by the public and/or registered visitors of the website. Wikipedia is the most well-known example of a wiki collaboration.

# X

XML Sitemap - A file for search engines that contains all of a domain's URLs. The file is used to help with indexing.

# Y

YouTube - The Internet's most popular community for sharing and hosting videos. Owned by Google, YouTube owns the distinction of being the second largest search engine online (behind Google itself). YouTube users, view, upload, like and comment on videos, and companies can pay to sponsor videos or advertise on popular YouTube channels.

# Index

## A

A/B Testing, 89, 111, 114, 117
Adwords, 85, 88, 89, 139
Affiliate Marketing, 126
Algorithm, 140-141
Amazon, 13-18, 103
Analytics,
> Web analytics, 66-70, 80
> Digital analytics, 66-70, 80, 150
Anchor Text, 141, 148

## B

B2B, 132
Backlink, 139, 148, 151
Black Hat Techniques, 139
Browser, 112, 117

## C

Clickthrough Rate (CTR), 89
Conversion, 78, 89-95, 104, 117
Conversion Rate, 78, 86, 90-95, 201
Customer Relationship Management (CRM), 108, 116
Call-to-Action, 33, 89

## D

Digital Analytics, 66-70, 80, 150
Digital Marketing,
> eCommerce, 12-15, 104, 121
> Mobile marketing & digital marketing, 30-41
> Social media & digital marketing, 50-63
> Web analytics & digital marketing, 66-70, 80
> Search marketing & digital marketing, 84-95

Email marketing & digital marketing, 102-120
Digital marketing sales, 120-135
SEO & digital marketing, 138-152
Getting noticed in digital marketing, 154-165
Digital marketer career advice, 170-183
Digital marketing in agency life, 186-192
Digital marketing educational opportunities, 194-206

E

eCommerce, 12-15, 104, 121
Email Marketing, 102-120
Engagement, 39, 55, 75, 106, 116

F

Facebook, 36, 50-54, 87
Funnel, 75

G

Godin, Seth, 46, 105, 182
Google, 19, 69, 70, 85, 139
Google Adwords, 85, 88
Google Algorithms, 140-141
Google Analytics, 69, 71, 79, 80
Google Search Console, 147
Google Webmaster Tools, 147-148

H

Hashtag, 63
HTTP, 74-80

I

Inbound Marketing, 51, 149-150, 175
Indexing, 147

Influencer, 5, 55, 105, 111, 122, 186-189
Instagram, 50-52, 67

## J

Job Search, 39, 63, 155, 170
Job Applicants, 156-164

## K

Key Performance Indicators (KPI), 41, 61, 75-78, 114
Keyword, 22, 85-88, 96
Keyword Optimization, 151
Keyword Stuffing, 139, 141

## L

Landing Page, 89. 175
Link, 33, 88
LinkedIn, 51, 52, 122
Linking Programs, 93

## M

Marketing Automation, 14, 108, 116
Meta Tags, 147-148
Mobile Marketing, 30-41

## N

Networking, 122

## O

Opt-In, 36, 39, 48, 104-106
Organic Link Building, 139
Organic Search, 143, 147-149
Organic Traffic, 143-145

P

Paid Search, 39, 76, 96, 139
Pay-Per-Click (PPC), 85, 87
Profile, 58, 98, 148, 155

R

Ranking, 70, 88, 140-150
Results Page, 70
Response Rate, 111
Retargeting, 86, 91, 116
Return on Investment (ROI), 78

S

Search Engine, 86-88, 91-96
Search Engine Marketing (SEM), 39, 85
Search Engine Optimization (SEO), 139-145
Search Term, 70, 86, 96, 151
Social Media Marketing, 51-63
Social Network, 15, 51
Spam, 37, 105,109, 114

T

Tag, 140, 148
Title Tag, 140
Traffic, 34, 71, 91, 143
Twitter, 36, 51-55, 63, 122, 179

U

Unsubscribe, 39
URL, 140, 148
User, 19, 32, 88
        Target User, 35, 113
        Mobile Users, 38-39

End User, 40, 45

V

Visitor, 67, 86

W

Walmart, 13-14, 68
Web Analytics, 66-70, 80

Y

YouTube, 5, 52-54

# References

1. https://www.gartner.com/smarterwithgartner/gartner-cmo-spend-survey-2016-2017-shows-marketing-budgets-continue-to-climb/, 7.

2. https://www.siliconrepublic.com/careers/150000-digital-jobs-forecast-but-few-have-the-skills-to-fill-them, 7.

3. https://digiday.com/partners/digital-marketers-love-and-hate-their-jobs/, 8.

4. https://www.emarketer.com/Article/US-Digital-Ad-Spending-Surpass-TV-this-Year/1014469, 8.

5. http://adage.com/article/digital/digital-ad-revenue-surpasses-tv-desktop-iab/308808/, 8.

6. http://www.dmnews.com/marketing-strategy/cmos-declare-2013-the-year-of-digital/article/270989/, 8.

7. http://martechseries.com/mts-insights/interviews/interview-rohit-prabhakar-head-digital-marketing-technology-mckesson/, 9.

8. https://www.glassdoor.com/blog/25-jobs-worklife-balance-2015/, 10.

9. https://www.entrepreneur.com/article/270139, 10.

10. https://www.inc.com/dave-kerpen/11-powerful-quotes-to-inspire-your-team-to-embrace-change.html, 10.

11. https://www.emarketer.com/Article/Retail-Sales-Worldwide-Will-Top-22-Trillion-This-Year/1011765, 11.

12. https://www.digitalcommerce360.com/2016/02/17/us-e-commerce-grows-146-2015/, 11.

13. https://www.digitalcommerce360.com/2017/02/17/us-e-commerce-sales-grow-156-2016/, 11.

14. http://wwd.com/business-news/financial/amazon-walmart-top-ecommerce-retailers-10383750/, 11.

15. https://news.walmart.com/2016/08/08/walmart-agrees-to-acquire-jetcom-one-of-the-fastest-growing-e-commerce-companies-in-the-us, 11.

16. https://www.cnbc.com/2013/11/18/us-online-shoppers-overtake-real-buyers-for-first-time.html, 12.

17. https://www.cnbc.com/2017/05/30/amazon-shares-hit-1000.html, 12.

18. https://www.drip.co/blog/tips-and-tactics/lifecycle-marketing/, 12.

19. http://variety.com/2017/digital/news/streaming-services-us-music-revenue-2016-1202019504/, 13.

20. http://fortune.com/2016/04/12/digital-music-sales-report/, 13.

21. https://techcrunch.com/2015/06/02/6-1b-smartphone-users-globally-by-2020-overtaking-basic-fixed-phone-subscriptions/, 13.

22. https://www.inc.com/jonathan-lacoste/3-digital-marketing-trends-retail-ecommerce-2016.html, 13.

23. http://www.businessinsider.com/beacons-impact-billions-in-reail-sales-2015-2, 13.

24. https://www.umbel.com/blog/mobile/15-companies-using-beacon-technology/, 13.

25. http://www.gigya.com/blog/5-stats-that-prove-businesses-must-personalize-to-win-customers/, 14.

26. https://techcrunch.com/2015/06/02/6-1b-smartphone-users-globally-by-2020-overtaking-basic-fixed-phone-subscriptions/, 19.

27. http://www.pewinternet.org/fact-sheet/mobile/, 19.

28. https://www.digitalturbine.com/blog/starbucks-a-case-study-in-effective-mobile-app-marketing/, 20.

29. https://www.marketingsociety.com/the-library/2013-highly-commended-mcdonalds-mobile-marketing-case-study, 21.

30. https://www.bloomberg.com/news/articles/2015-06-18/america-s-most-hated-dinnertime-interruption-is-facing-new-test, 21.

31. https://www.salesforce.com/blog/2016/03/successful-mobile-marketing-campaigns-tips-small-businesses.html, 22.

32. http://www.businessinsider.com/e-commerce-impulse-buy-category-2015-11, 22.

33. https://www.networkworld.com/article/3092446/smartphones/we-touch-our-phones-2617-times-a-day-says-study.html, 23.

34. http://time.com/4147614/smartphone-usage-us-2015/, 23.

35. http://www.smartinsights.com/mobile-marketing/mobile-advertising/7-effective-mobile-marketing-campaigns/, 23.

36. https://www.tune.com/blog/secrets-of-successful-mobile-marketing-campaigns-interview-with-mosaics-leslie-albertson-pb14/, 25.

37. https://venturebeat.com/2012/10/20/zuck-startup-school/, 28.

38. http://money.cnn.com/2016/04/28/investing/facebook-trillion-dollar-market-value/, 28.

39. http://money.cnn.com/2016/04/28/investing/facebook-trillion-dollar-market-value/, 28.

40. http://www.socialmediaexaminer.com/social-media-research-shows-what-people-expect-from-brands/, 28.

41. https://www.slideshare.net/HubSpot/the-social-lifecycle-consumer-insights-to-improve-your-business, 28.

42. http://www.nielsen.com/eu/en/press-room/2015/recommendations-from-friends-remain-most-credible-form-of-advertising.html, 28.

43. https://www.theguardian.com/technology/2005/aug/29/mondaymediasection.blogging, 29.

44. http://customerthink.com/you_can_learn_dell_hell_dell_did/, 29.

45. https://www.symmetricalmm.com/single-post/2016/12/22/Social-Media-Marketing-for-Small-Businesses-An-Interview-with-Mel-Welsh, 30.

46. http://www.cyberalert.com/blog/index.php/b2b-companies-endanger-their-growth-by-neglecting-social-media-marketing/, 31.

47. http://blog.careercloud.com/post/55175638420/9-social-media-job-search-success-stories, 35.

48. https://ca.linkedin.com/in/jaffery, 35.

49. https://money.usnews.com/careers/best-jobs/rankings/the-100-best-jobs,35.

50. http://www.bernhart.com/digital-analytics-a-career-of-the-future/,35.

51. https://www.kaushik.net/avinash/web-analytics-career-guide-job-strategy/, 36.

52. http://keyhole.co/blog/measure-content-marketing-strategy-michael-brenner-interview/, 36.

53. http://bridg.com/blog/walmart-big-data/, 36.

54. https://delmainanalytics.com/case-studies/dani-weiss-photography/, 37.

55. http://searchcio.techtarget.com/opinion/Ten-big-data-case-studies-in-a-nutshell, 41.

56. https://www.kaushik.net/avinash/seven-skills-to-look-for-in-a-web-analytics-manager/, 41.

57. http://searchcio.techtarget.com/opinion/Ten-big-data-case-studies-in-a-nutshell, 42.

58. http://www.stern.nyu.edu/programs-admissions/ms business-analytics, 43.

59. https://www.emarketer.com/Article/US-Digital-Display-Ad-Spending-Surpass-Search-Ad-Spending-2016/1013442, 44.

60. https://www.mediapost.com/publications/article/286850/retail-advertisers-spent-144-billion-on-us-goo.html, 44.

61. http://www.zenithoptimedia.com/wp-content/uploads/2016/03/Adspend-forecasts-March-2016-executive-summary.pdf, 50.

62. https://digitalmarketinginstitute.com/blog/demand-digital-marketing-skills-2015, 50.

63. http://www.radicati.com/wp/wp-content/uploads/2015/02/Email-Statistics-Report-2015-2019-Executive-Summary.pdf, 53.

64. https://www.salesforce.com/blog/category/marketing.html?d=marketing-cloud.com/blog/91-of-consumers-use-email-at-least-daily/&internal=true, 53.

65. http://sethgodin.typepad.com/seths_blog/2009/02/email-campaign-case-studies-one-good-one-bad.html, 54.

66. https://tax.thomsonreuters.com/blog/the-importance-of-visual-content-marketing-infographic-2/, 54.

67. https://www.emailmonday.com/mobile-email-usage-statistics, 54.

68. http://www.dmnews.com/email-marketing/uber-go-bragh/article/483742/, 54.

69. https://theamericangenius.com/business-marketing/why-you-shouldnt-underestimate-the-value-of-email-marketing/, 54.

70. https://www.salesforce.com/products/marketing-cloud/overview/, 55.

71. https://www.merkleinc.com/news-and-events/press-releases/2011/merkle-publishes-view-digital-inbox-whitepaper#.U7rdNLGTE2J, 55.

72. https://www.getvero.com/resources/, 57.

73. https://www.groovehq.com/blog/growing-email-list, 57.

74. https://www.emailmonday.com/marketing-automation-statistics-overview, 60.

75. https://blog.wishpond.com/post/98235786280/50-a-b-split-test-conversion-optimization-case-studies, 61.

76. https://www.statista.com/topics/1386/digital-music/, 62.

77. http://www.gamesindustry.biz/articles/2017-01-06-steam-paid-game-revenue-flat-in-2016-despite-escalating-releases-steam-spy, 62.

78. https://www2.deloitte.com/content/dam/Deloitte/us/Documents/consumer-business/us-cb-navigating-the-new-digital-divide-v2-051315.pdf, 62.

79. https://networkingexchangeblog.att.com/, 62.

80. https://www.businessesgrow.com/2013/09/18/case-study-how-i-made-47-million-from-my-b2b-blog/, 63.

81. https://www.earlytorise.com/how-a-funeral-turned-joe-girard-into-the-worlds-greatest-salesperson/, 65.

82. http://fortune.com/2014/12/08/is-gary-vaynerchuk-vaynermedia-for-real/, 69.

83. http://blog.close.io/5-mega-successful-entrepreneurs-who-launched-their-careers-in-sales, 70.

84. https://quoteinvestigator.com/2014/05/04/adapt/, 71.

85. https://www.legalinsites.com/2016/09/23/major-changes-googles-penguin-algorithm/, 71.

86. https://moz.com/beginners-guide-to-seo/why-search-engine-marketing-is-necessary, 72.

87. https://moz.com/google-algorithm-change, 72.

88. https://www.conductor.com/blog/2015/03/seo-jobs-seo-salary-growth/, 72.

89. https://searchengineland.com/seo-industry-worth-65-billion-will-ever-stop-growing-248559, 72.

90. https://www.forbes.com/sites/steveolenski/2014/03/26/7-reasons-why-your-business-should-invest-in-seo/#6913403e2563, 72.

91. http://www.business2community.com/seo/case-studies-prove-seo-pertinent-businesses-01747061#U7U341ywURkJLdQc.97, 73.

92. http://dev.webtalentmarketing.com/seo/case-studies/home-improvement-small-business/, 73.

93. https://moz.com/beginners-guide-to-seo, 77.

94. https://www.link-assistant.com/blog/seo-career/, 78.

95. https://dazeinfo.com/2016/11/23/digital-marketing-career-salary/, 79.

96. https://digitalmarketinginstitute.com/blog/3-digital-marketing-interview-tips-help-land-dream-job, 79.

97. http://www.businessinsider.com/phrases-to-keep-off-your-linkedin-profile-2014-8, 80.

98. https://www.linkedin.com/in/ninamufleh, 80.

99. http://www.news18.com/news/india/21-yr-old-made-an-impressive-gq-style-resume-and-got-hired-without-an-interview-1258233.html, 81.

100. http://www.marketingdive.com/news/digital-marketing-skills-in-de-mand-recruiters/417884/, 81.

101. https://www.iwillteachyoutoberich.com/the-briefcase-technique/, 84.

102. https://news.stanford.edu/2005/06/14/jobs-061505/, 86.

103. http://www.marketinghire.com/, 86.

104. http://cressmedia.com/land-my-dream-job-bill-simmons-ringer/, 87.

105. http://cressmedia.com/rob-cressy-entrepreneurial-journey/, 87.

106. https://vtldesign.com/vital-design-news-jobs-and-culture/news-culture/how-i-used-an-inbound-marketing-strategy-to-land-my-dream-job/, 89.

107. https://www.nationalcareerfairs.com/, 89.

108. https://www.linkedin.com/pulse/digital-marketing-job-fair-nick-longo, 89.

109. http://www.cosmopolitan.com/career/interviews/a38342/get-that-life-shama-hyder-marketing-zen-group/, 90.

110. https://twitter.com/randfish, 90.

111. https://blog.hubspot.com/sales/landed-my-dream-job#sm.00001yfbbbhe-sue7vrittrag1j7sf, 91.

112. https://www.entrepreneur.com/article/253522, 93.

113. https://www.amazon.com/Chief-Marketing-Officers-at-Work/dp/1484219309/ref=as_li_ss_tl?ie=UTF8&linkCode=sl1&tag=joshsteim-le-20&linkId=2e11aca5ef9c3886d8e90d4bd6166772, 93.

114. https://www.entrepreneur.com/article/287821, 93.

115. https://digitalmarketinginstitute.com/blog/digital-marketing-agency-brand-choose-job-youll-love, 93.

116. https://www.glassdoor.com/blog/digital-agency-work/, 94.

117. https://www.onlinemarketinginstitute.org/blog/2015/01/top-20-digi-tal-marketing-strategists-for-2015/, 95.

118. https://agencymanagementinstitute.com/rohit-bhargava/, 95.

119. Sources used for Chapter 13 were referenced from current information on certification, college and university websites (97-101).

56816572R00150

Made in the USA
Columbia, SC
02 May 2019